OCS EIS/EA
MMS 2007-059

Proposed Gulf of Mexico OCS Oil and Gas Lease Sale 206

I0411760

Central Planning Area

Environmental Assessment

Author

Minerals Management Service
Gulf of Mexico OCS Region

U.S. Department of the Interior
Minerals Management Service
Gulf of Mexico OCS Region

New Orleans
October 2007

FINDING OF NO NEW SIGNIFICANT IMPACT

The U.S. Department of the Interior, Minerals Management Service (MMS) has prepared an environmental assessment (EA) for proposed Lease Sale 206 in the Central Planning Area (CPA) of the Gulf of Mexico (GOM) Outer Continental Shelf (OCS) to determine whether MMS can make a Finding of No New Significant Impact (FONNSI) or should prepare a supplemental environmental impact statement (EIS).

In April 2007, MMS filed with the U.S. Environmental Protection Agency a Final EIS covering CPA Lease Sales 205, 206, 208, 213, 216, and 222; and Western Planning Area Lease Sales 204, 207, 210, 215, and 218 in the GOM (Multisale EIS). Because the Multisale EIS examined the environmental impacts of a sale similar in size, nature, and potential level of development as proposed Lease Sale 206, the EA tiers off the Multisale EIS and incorporates much of the material by reference. It also reexamines the potential environmental effects of proposed Lease Sale 206 and the alternatives based on any new information regarding potential impacts or issues that were not available at the time the Multisale EIS was prepared.

The purpose of the EA is to analyze whether new information indicates that there are likely to be significant new impacts that were not addressed in the Multisale EIS. As part of the scoping process for the EA, MMS researched and reviewed new information to determine if any resources should be reevaluated or if the new information would alter conclusions of the Multisale EIS. No new information was found that would necessitate a reanalysis of the impacts of proposed Lease Sale 206 upon environmental or socioeconomic resources. The analyses and potential impacts detailed in the Multisale EIS apply for proposed Lease Sale 206. New information was found that further supports or elaborates on analyses or information presented in the Multisale EIS, but it does not change the conclusions of any of the analyses in the Multisale EIS.

Based on the analyses in the EA, no new significant impacts were identified for proposed Lease Sale 206 that were not already assessed in the Multisale EIS, nor is it necessary to change the conclusions of the kinds, levels, or locations of impacts described in that document. Therefore, MMS has determined that a supplemental EIS is not required and is issuing this FONNSI.

Supporting Document

Gulf of Mexico OCS Oil and Gas Lease Sales: 2007-2012; Western Planning Area Sales 204, 207, 210, 215, and 218; Central Planning Area Sales 205, 206, 208, 213, 216, and 222—Final Environmental Impact Statement; Volumes I and II (USDOI, MMS, 2007a) (available upon request)

_____
Director

10-22-07
_____
Date

TABLE OF CONTENTS

FIGURES

Page

TABLES

Page

1. OBJECTIVES OF THE ENVIRONMENTAL ASSESSMENT

This environmental assessment (EA) addresses one proposed Federal action: oil and gas Lease Sale 206 in the proposed lease sale area of the Central Planning Area (CPA) of the Gulf of Mexico (GOM) Outer Continental Shelf (OCS) as scheduled in the *Outer Continental Shelf Oil and Gas Leasing Program 2007-2012* (5-Year Program) (USDOI, MMS, 2007b). This EA incorporates by reference all of the relevant material in the Multisale environmental impact statement (EIS) from which it tiers (*Gulf of Mexico OCS Oil and Gas Lease Sales: 2007-2012; Western Planning Area Sales 204, 207, 210, 215, and 218; Central Planning Area Sales 205, 206, 208, 213, 216, and 222—Final Environmental Impact Statement; Volumes I and II* (Multisale EIS) (USDOI, MMS, 2007a). The EA has been prepared to aid in the determination of whether or not new available information indicates that the proposed lease sale would result in new significant impacts not addressed in the Multisale EIS.

In preparation for this EA, the U.S. Department of the Interior (USDOI), Minerals Management Service (MMS) reexamined the potential environmental effects of proposed Lease Sale 206 and the alternatives based on any new information regarding potential impacts and issues not available at the time MMS published the Multisale EIS in April 2007. New information was reviewed to determine if any resources should be reevaluated or if the new information would alter conclusions of the Multisale EIS. No new information was found that would necessitate a reanalysis of the impacts of proposed Lease Sale 206 upon any of the environmental or socioeconomic resources. The analyses and potential impacts detailed in the Multisale EIS apply for proposed Lease Sale 206. New information was found that further supports or elaborates on the analyses or information presented in the Multisale EIS, but it does not change the conclusions of any of the analyses in the Multisale EIS.

Federal regulations allow for an agency to analyze related or similar proposals in one EIS (40 CFR 1502.4). Since CPA Lease Sales 205, 206, 208, 213, 216, and 222 and their projected activities are very similar, if not almost identical, MMS prepared a single EIS for the six lease sales. The Multisale EIS approach focuses the National Environmental Policy Act (NEPA) EIS process on the differences between the proposed lease sales and new information and issues. Although the Multisale EIS addressed six proposed CPA lease sale actions, the Secretary of the Interior (Secretary) makes a separate decision for each lease sale.

The Multisale EIS can be obtained from the Minerals Management Service, Gulf of Mexico OCS Region, Attention: Public Information Office (MS 5034), 1201 Elmwood Park Boulevard, Room 114, New Orleans, Louisiana 70123-2394 (1-800-200-GULF) or viewed on the MMS website at http://www.gomr.mms.gov. A list of libraries that have copies of the Multisale EIS and their locations is also available on the MMS Internet website.

2. PURPOSE OF AND NEED FOR THE PROPOSED ACTION

Purpose of the Proposed Action

The purpose of this proposed action (CPA Lease Sale 206) is to offer for lease all unleased blocks in the proposed lease sale area (**Figure 1**) that may contain economically recoverable oil and natural gas resources. The proposed lease sale would provide qualified bidders the opportunity to bid upon and lease acreage in the proposed lease sale area in order to explore, develop, and produce oil and natural gas.

Need for the Proposed Action

The GOM constitutes one of the world's major oil- and gas-producing areas and has proved to be a steady and reliable source of crude oil and natural gas for more than 50 years. Oil from the GOM would help reduce the Nation's need for oil imports and reduce the environmental risks associated with oil tankering. Natural gas is generally considered to be an environmentally preferable alternative to oil in terms of both production and consumption.

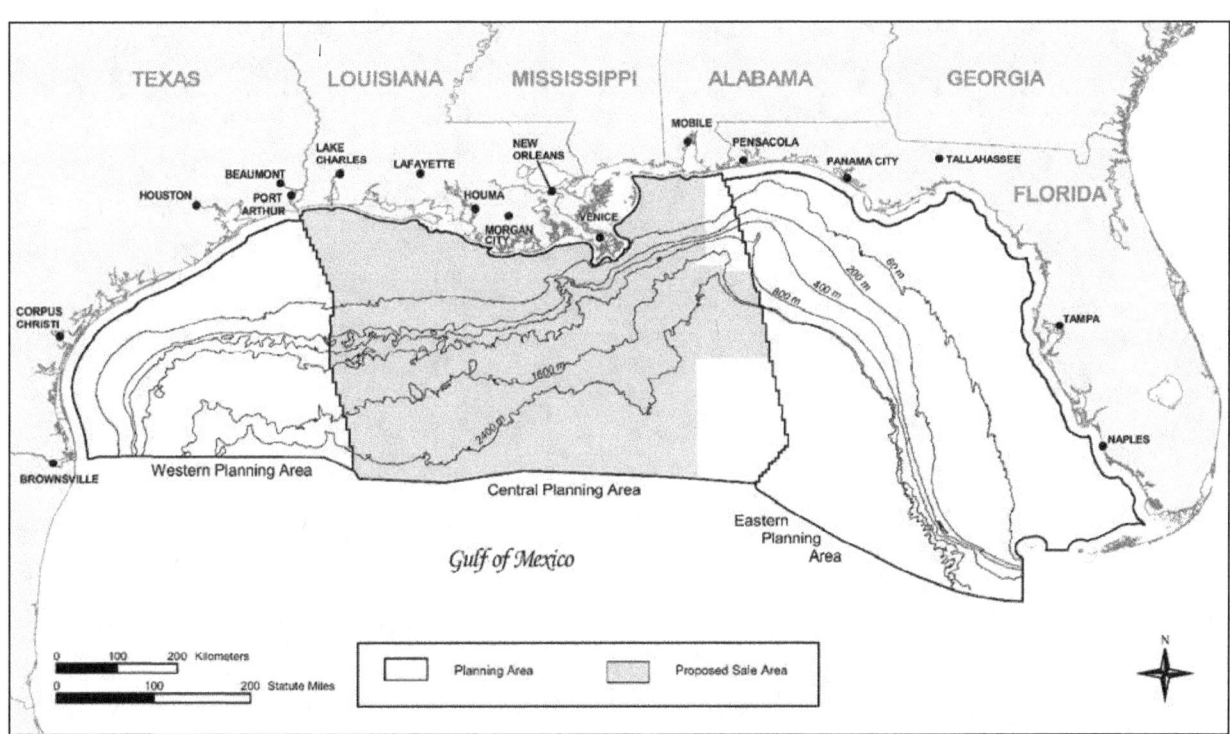

Figure 1. Gulf of Mexico Outer Continental Shelf Planning Areas, Proposed Lease Sale Area, and Locations of Major Cities.

3. ALTERNATIVES INCLUDING THE PROPOSED ACTION

3.1. ALTERNATIVE A—PROPOSED ACTION

Alternative A (Preferred Alternative)—The Proposed Action: This alternative would offer for lease all unleased blocks within the CPA for oil and gas operations (**Figure 2**), with the following exceptions:

(1) blocks that were previously included within the Eastern Planning Area (EPA) and that are within 100 mi of the Florida coast;

(2) blocks that were previously included within the EPA and that were previously under Presidential as well as subject to annual Congressional moratoria;

(3) blocks that are beyond the U.S. Exclusive Economic Zone in the area known as the northern portion of the Eastern Gap; and

(4) whole and partial blocks that lie within the 1.4-nmi buffer zone north of the continental shelf boundary between the U.S. and Mexico for Sales 205, 206, 208, and 213 only.

The CPA sale area encompasses about 58.7 million ac of the CPA's 66.3 million ac. The estimated amount of resources projected to be developed as a result of any one proposed CPA lease sale is 0.776-1.292 billion barrels of oil (BBO) and 3.236-5.229 trillion cubic feet (Tcf) of gas.

The analyses of impacts summarized below and described in detail in Chapters 4.2.2 and 4.4 of the Multisale EIS are based on the development scenario, which is a set of assumptions and estimates on the amounts, locations, and timing for OCS exploration, development, and production operations and facilities, both offshore and onshore. A detailed discussion of the development scenario and major related impact-producing factors is included in Chapters 4.1.1, 4.1.2, and 4.3 of the Multisale EIS.

Figure 2. Location of Proposed Stipulations and Deferrals.

3.2. ALTERNATIVES TO THE PROPOSED ACTION

Alternative B—The Proposed Action Excluding the Unleased Blocks Near Biologically Sensitive Topographic Features: This alternative would offer for lease all unleased blocks in the CPA, as described for the proposed action, with the exception of any unleased blocks subject to the Topographic Features Stipulation. A detailed analysis of Alternative B is presented in Chapter 4.2.2.2 of the Final Multisale EIS.

Alternative C—The Proposed Action Excluding the Unleased Blocks Within 15 Miles of the Baldwin County, Alabama, Coast: This alternative would offer for lease all unleased blocks in the CPA, as described for the proposed action, with the exception of any unleased blocks within 15 mi of the Baldwin County, Alabama, coast. A detailed analysis of Alternative C is presented in Chapter 4.2.2.3 of the Final Multisale EIS.

Alternative D—Use of a Nomination and Tract Selection Leasing System: A detailed analysis of Alternative D is presented in Chapter 4.2.2.4 of the Final Multisale EIS. This alternative addressed a very specific scenario that would limit the number of blocks offered for lease for proposed Lease Sale 206, potentially reducing the number of blocks leased.

Since the publication of the Final Multisale EIS, MMS has awarded a contract to an outside contractor to study alternative approaches to leasing that may serve better the many goals of the OCSLA. This MMS-funded study, in conjunction with MMS review and assessment of its policy implications, is expected to take 2-3 years. The MMS will provide the contractor with all of the comments received on alternatives to areawide leasing. If it is determined that one or more alternative approaches to leasing is preferable, the 5-Year Program could be adjusted accordingly or it can be incorporated into the subsequent 5-Year Program.

Until the study and its assessment are complete, MMS must be cautious regarding the effects that any policy changes might have on the achievement of other statutory and implicit goals of the Federal OCS Program. Among these goals are expeditious and orderly development of the natural resources of the OCS and maintaining a diverse and competitive industry. Areawide leasing allows smaller independent companies to timely acquire and rapidly produce low-resource, low-risk fields, while inducing larger companies to develop state-of-the-art technology to explore and develop deepwater prospects. It also encourages strong and innovative seismic exploration and geophysical contracting and processing industries. In addition, a sudden change in policy that restricts access to oil and gas resources or that alters the timetables the offshore industry has come to expect and depend upon may lead to undesirable socioeconomic disruptions in local coastal economies.

Alternative E—No Action: This alternative is the cancellation of CPA Lease Sale 206. The opportunity for development of the estimated 0.776-1.292 BBO and 3.236-5.229 Tcf of gas that could have resulted from a proposed CPA lease sale would be precluded or postponed. Any potential environmental impacts resulting from a proposed lease sale would not occur or would be postponed. Other sources of energy would substitute for the lost production. Principal substitutes would be additional imports, conservation, additional domestic production, and switching to other fuels. These alternatives, except conservation, have significant negative environmental impacts of their own, which are analyzed in the Final EIS for the 5-Year Program (USDOI, MMS, 2007c).

The MMS recently published a report that examined previous exploration and development activity scenarios (USDOI, MMS, 2007d). The MMS compared forecasted activity with the actual activity that has resulted in 14 Western Planning Area (WPA) and 14 Central Planning Area lease sales.

The report shows that many lease sales contribute to the present level of OCS activity, and any single lease sale accounts for only a small percentage of the total OCS activities. In 2006, leases from 92 different sales contributed to GOM production, while an average CPA lease sale contributed to 2 percent of oil production and 2 percent of gas production in the CPA. In 2006, leases from 15 different sales contributed to the installation of production structures in the GOM, while an average CPA lease sale contributed to 6 percent of the installation of production structures in the CPA. In 2006, leases from 70 different sales contributed to wells drilled in the GOM, while an average CPA lease sale contributed to 4 percent of wells drilled in the CPA.

Like other lease sales, Lease Sale 206 would contribute to maintaining the present level of OCS activity in the Gulf of Mexico. Exploration and development activity, including service-vessel trips, helicopter trips, and construction, that would result from Lease Sale 206 would replace activity resulting from existing leases that have reached or are near the end of their economic life.

If Lease Sale 206 would be cancelled, the resulting development of oil and gas would most likely be postponed to a future sale; therefore, the overall level of OCS activity in the CPA would only be reduced by a small percentage, if any.

3.3. MITIGATION MEASURES

Proposed Lease Sale 206 and all subsequent activities resulting from it are subject to the existing regulations and proposed lease stipulations designed to reduce environmental risks. Lease stipulations are legally binding restrictions and operating requirements that, if adopted, become part of lease contracts. The Multisale EIS analyzed seven stipulations proposed to be applied to leases resulting from CPA Lease Sale 206: Topographic Features Stipulation; the Live Bottom Stipulation; the Military Areas Stipulation; the Evacuation Stipulation; the Coordination Stipulation; the Blocks South of Baldwin County, Alabama, Stipulation; and the Protected Species Stipulation. Chapter 2.4.1.3 of the Multisale EIS discusses the effectiveness of these stipulations. Additional stipulations or mitigation requirements to be included in Lease Sale 206 will be described in the Final Notice of Sale for Lease Sale 206.

3.3.1. Summary of Stipulations Discussed in the Multisale EIS

Seven environmental and military mitigations, referred to as lease stipulations, were included for analysis in the Multisale EIS. These stipulations were developed as the result of scoping efforts over a number of years for the continuing OCS Program in the GOM. These stipulations and their effectiveness are described in more detail in Chapter 2 of the Multisale EIS. Any stipulations or mitigation requirements to be included in Lease Sale 206 will be described in detail in the Final Notice of Sale for Lease Sale 206. Stipulations or mitigations requirements, in addition to those analyzed in the Multisale EIS, can also be developed and applied, and they will also be described in detail in the Final Notice of Sale.

The following environmental and military stipulations are applicable to Lease Sale 206:

- The **Topographic Features Stipulation** protects the biota of the topographic features from adverse effects due to routine oil and gas activities, including physical damage from anchoring and rig emplacement and the potential toxic and smothering effects from muds and cuttings discharges. The Topographic Features Stipulation has been included in leases since 1973 and has effectively prevented damage to the biota of these banks from routine oil and gas activities such as anchoring. Monitoring studies have demonstrated that the shunting requirements of the stipulation are effective in preventing the muds and cuttings from impacting the biota of the banks. Although deferral of blocks with topographic features has been analyzed as an alternative in EIS's and EA's for all recent WPA and CPA sales, this alternative has never been selected. The topographic highs on and near these blocks are often associated with salt domes, which are attractive areas for hydrocarbon exploration. Instead, blocks on the topographic features have been offered for lease with a stipulation that has proven effective in protecting sensitive biological resources.

- The **Military Areas Stipulation** has been applied to all blocks leased in military areas since 1977 and reduces potential impacts, particularly in regards to safety, but does not reduce or eliminate the actual physical presence of oil and gas operations in areas where military operations are conducted. The stipulation contains a "hold harmless" clause (holding the U.S. Government harmless in case of accident involving military operations) and requires lessees to coordinate their activities with appropriate local military contacts.

- The **Protected Species Stipulation** has been applied to all blocks leased in the GOM since December 2001. This stipulation was developed in consultation with the U.S. Department of Commerce (USDOC), National Oceanic and Atmospheric

Administration (NOAA), National Marine Fisheries Service (NMFS), and U.S. Fish and Wildlife Service (FWS) in accordance with Section 7 of the Endangered Species Act of 1973 (ESA) and is designed to minimize or avoid potential adverse impacts to federally protected species.

- The **Live Bottom (Pinnacle Trend) Stipulation** covers a small portion of the northeastern CPA sale area that is characterized by a pinnacle trend, which is classified as a live bottom under the stipulation. The MMS developed the stipulation to protect biological resources in the Pinnacle Trend in response to concerns that disturbing any of the series of topographic irregularities might adversely affect biological communities that have developed on the surfaces of the features and affect the habitat they provide for pelagic fishes. The stipulation requires avoidance of the features during the placement of oil and gas structures and the laying of pipelines. The stipulation has been adopted in CPA sales since 1990 and has been effective in protecting the features and resident biological communities from damage.

- The **Evacuation Stipulation** would apply to any lease in the easternmost portion of the CPA sale area. This stipulation was developed in consultation with the U.S. Department of Defense (DOD) to address specific potential use conflict issues between oil and gas operations and military operations in the GOM. An evacuation stipulation has been applied to all blocks leased in this area since 2001. This stipulation would provide for the evacuation of personnel and the shut-in of operations during any events conducted by the military that could pose a danger to ongoing oil and gas operations. It is expected that these measures will serve to eliminate dangerous conflicts between oil and gas operations and military operations.

- The **Coordination Stipulation** would apply to any lease in the easternmost portion of the CPA sale area. This stipulation was developed in consultation with DOD to address specific potential use conflict issues between oil and gas operations and military operations in the GOM. A coordination stipulation has been applied to all blocks leased in this area since 2001. This stipulation would provide for the review of pending oil and gas operations by military authorities and could result in delaying oil and gas operations if military activities have been scheduled in the area that may put the oil and gas operations and personnel at risk.

- The **Blocks South of Baldwin County, Alabama, Stipulation** will be included only on leases south of and within 15 mi of Baldwin County, Alabama. For several years, the Governor of Alabama has continually indicated opposition to new leasing south and within 15 mi of Baldwin County but has requested that, if the area is offered for lease, a lease stipulation to reduce the potential for visual impacts be applied to all new leases in this area. Prior to the decision in 1999 on the Final Notice of Sale for Sale 172, the MMS, GOM OCS Regional Director, in consultation with the Geological Survey of Alabama/State Oil and Gas Board, developed a lease stipulation to be applied to any new leases within the 15-mi area to mitigate potential visual impacts. The stipulation specifies requirements for consultation that lessees must follow when developing plans for fixed structures. The stipulation has been continually adopted in annual Central GOM lease sales since 1999.

3.3.2. Existing Mitigations

Chapter 2.2.2.2 of the Multisale EIS discusses mitigations that would be applied by MMS. Mitigations have been proposed, identified, evaluated, or developed through previous MMS lease sale NEPA review and analysis. Many of these mitigations have been adopted and incorporated into regulations and/or guidelines governing OCS exploration, development, and production activities. The MMS rigorously reviews all plans for OCS activities (e.g., exploration and development plans, pipeline applications, and structure-removal applications) to ensure compliance with established laws and regulations. Existing mitigations must be incorporated and documented in plans submitted to MMS. The

MMS enforces operational compliance with these mitigations through the MMS on-site inspection program.

Mitigations that are a standard part of the MMS program ensure that the operations are always conducted in an environmentally sound manner. For example, mitigations ensure that site-clearance procedures eliminate potential snags to commercial fishing nets and require surveys to detect and avoid archaeological sites and biologically-sensitive areas such as pinnacles, topographic features, and chemosynthetic communities.

Some MMS-identified mitigations are incorporated into OCS operations through cooperative agreements or efforts with industry and various State and Federal agencies. These mitigations include NMFS' Observer Program to protect marine mammals and sea turtles during explosive removals, labeling operational supplies to track possible sources of accidental debris loss, development of methods of pipeline landfall to eliminate impacts to barrier beaches, and semiannual beach cleanup events.

Site-specific mitigations are also applied by MMS during plan reviews. The MMS determined that many of these site-specific mitigations were consistently applied and used these to develop a list of "standard" mitigations. There are currently over 120 standard mitigations. The wording of a standard mitigation is developed by MMS in advance and may be applied whenever conditions warrant. Standard mitigation text is revised as often as necessary (e.g., to reflect changes in regulatory citations, agency/personnel contact numbers, and internal policy). Site-specific mitigation categories air quality, archaeological resources, artificial reef material, chemosynthetic communities, Flower Garden Banks, topographic features, hard bottoms/pinnacles, military warning areas and Eglin water test areas, Naval mine warfare areas, hydrogen sulfide, drilling hazards, remotely operated vehicle surveys, geophysical survey reviews, and general safety concerns. Site-specific mitigation types include advisories, conditions of approval, hazard survey reviews, inspection requirements, notifications, post-approval submittals, reminders, and safety precautions. In addition to standard mitigations, MMS may also apply nonrecurring mitigations that are developed on a case-by-case basis.

3.3.3. Notices to Lessees and Operators

The MMS issues Notices to Lessees and Operators (NTL's) to provide clarification, description, or interpretation of a regulation; to provide guidelines on the implementation of a special lease stipulation or regional requirement; or to convey administrative information. A detailed listing of current GOM OCS Region NTL's is available through the MMS, GOM OCS Region's Internet website at http://www.gomr.mms.gov/homepg/regulate/regs/ntls/ntl_lst.html or through the Region's Public Information Office at (504) 736-2519 or 1-800-200-GULF. The MMS issued several NTL's related to the 2007 hurricane season, which are discussed in **Chapter 4.1.3**. Several NTL's requiring monitoring are described in the following section.

3.3.4. Monitoring

The MMS requires post-activity submittals for several activities, including seismic surveys and installation and decommissioning operations. Post-activity submittals allow MMS to monitor compliance with mitigations and to determine the effectiveness of those mitigations. The MMS is continually revising applicable mitigations to allow the GOM Region to more easily and routinely track mitigation compliance and effectiveness. A primary focus of this effort is requiring post-approval submittal of information within a specified timeframe after a triggering event that is currently tracked by MMS (e.g., end of operations reports for plans, construction reports for pipelines, and removal reports for structure removals).

In addition to compliance monitoring, MMS's Environmental Studies and Research Monitoring involves a repeated sampling of the environment over time to establish baseline conditions, determine natural variability, and assess changes and trends due to human activities. The MMS either conducts or requires this type of monitoring through its Environmental Studies Program to determine the extent to which activities caused by or permitted by MMS, such as development of offshore oil and gas, sand and gravel, and methane hydrate resources, affect the human, marine, and coastal environments. As a part of the Environmental Studies Program, the GOM Region has funded more than 350 completed or ongoing environmental studies.

The following describes some of these monitoring activities.

Protected Species NTL's

The Protected Species Stipulation is embodied in NTL's 2007-G02, 2007-G03, and 2007-G04, which instruct lessees and operators on how to implement these mitigations.

Implementation of Seismic Survey Mitigation Measures and Protected Species Observer Program (NTL 2007-G02)

NTL 2007-G02, "Implementation of Seismic Survey Mitigation Measures and Protected Species Observer Program," details information on ramp-up procedures, observation methods, and reporting requirements to be followed by the seismic industry during certain geological and geophysical survey operations. The conditions prescribed under the NTL aid in reducing the chance of harassment to nearby marine mammals and sea turtles. The report data received from the companies is being used by MMS to monitor the effectiveness of current mitigations.

Marine Trash and Debris Awareness and Elimination (NTL 2007-G03)

NTL 2007-G03, "Marine Trash and Debris Awareness and Elimination," provides guidance to prevent intentional and/or accidental introduction of debris into the marine environment. Operators are prohibited from deliberately discharging containers and other similar materials (i.e., trash and debris) into the marine environment (30 CFR 250.300(a) and (b)(6)) and are required to make durable identification markings on equipment, tools, containers (especially drums), and other material (30 CFR 250.300(c)). An annual report that describes the marine trash and debris awareness training process and certifies that the training process has been followed for the previous calendar year is to be provided to MMS by January 31 of each year.

Vessel Strike Avoidance and Injured/Dead Protected Species Reporting (NTL 2007-G04)

NTL 2007-G04, "Vessel Strike Avoidance and Injured/Dead Protected Species Reporting," explains how operators must implement measures to minimize the risk of vessel strikes to protected species and report observations of injured or dead protected species. Vessel operators and crews must maintain a vigilant watch for marine protected species and slow down or stop their vessel to avoid striking protected species. Crews must report sightings of any injured or dead protected species (marine mammals and sea turtles) immediately, regardless of whether the injury or death is caused by their vessel, to the Marine Mammal and Sea Turtle Stranding Hotline or the Marine Mammal Stranding Network. In addition, if it was their own vessel that collided with a protected species, MMS must be notified within 24 hours of the strike.

The importance of accurate and complete reporting of the results of the mitigations cannot be overstated. Only through diligent and careful reporting can MMS, and subsequently NMFS, determine the need for and effectiveness of mitigations. Information on observer effort and seismic operations are as important as animal sighting and behavior data.

Biologically Sensitive Areas of the Gulf of Mexico (NTL 2004-G05)

The Live Bottom (Pinnacle Trend) Stipulation and Topographic Features Stipulation are embodied in the comprehensive NTL 2004-G05, "Biologically Sensitive Areas of the Gulf of Mexico." In addition to existing stipulated areas for biological features, this NTL establishes a new category of protected area termed "Potentially Sensitive Biological Features." These are hard-bottom features not protected by a biological lease stipulation that are of moderate to high relief (about 8 ft (2.4 m) or higher), provide surface area for the growth of sessile invertebrates, and have the potential to attract large numbers of fish. These features would be located outside any "No Activity Zone" of any of the named topographic features (banks) or the 70 live-bottom (pinnacle trend) stipulated blocks. Following the completion of any activity that proposed disturbance of the seafloor within a specified distance of pinnacles, live-bottom (low-relief) features, or potentially sensitive biological features, operators must submit a map showing the location of the seafloor disturbance relative to these features.

Site Clearance (NTL 98-26)

NTL 98-26, "Minimum Interim Requirements for Site Clearance (and Verification) of Abandoned Oil and Gas Structures in the GOM," provides the requirements and guidelines for removing bottom debris and gear after structure decommissioning and removal operations. These mitigations ensure that site-clearance procedures eliminate potential snags to commercial fishing nets and require surveys to detect and avoid archaeological sites and biologically-sensitive areas such as pinnacles, topographic features, and chemosynthetic communities.

Once all bottom-founded components are severed and the structures/wells are removed, operators must verify that the seafloor is clear of obstructions and the site has been returned to prelease conditions. Site-clearance verification must take place within 60 days after structure-removal operations have been conducted. Procedures include sonar surveys and/or trawling the cleared site by a licensed "shrimp" trawler to ensure that no "hangs" exist.

Remotely Operated Vehicle Surveys (NTL 2003-G03)

On January 23, 2003, MMS issued NTL 2003-G03, "Remotely Operated Vehicle (ROV) Surveys in Deepwater." The NTL requires ROV surveys and reports in water depths greater than 400 m (1,312 ft). Eighteen grid areas were developed to ensure a broad and systematic analysis of deep water and to depict areas of biological similarity, primarily on the basis of benthic communities. The grid areas cover the WPA sale area and CPA sale area, with the exception of the easternmost portion.

Operators must submit a ROV survey plan with each exploration plan submitted in each grid area and with the Development Operations Coordination Document for the first surface structure proposed in each grid area. The ROV surveys will serve several purposes. In addition to monitoring the effects of the particular plans for which they are required, the surveys will improve our overall knowledge of benthic habitats in deep water and provide more information on the seafloor in deep water. The surveys will also provide information on the distribution and accumulation of muds and cuttings and thereby possibly help us to develop and refine mitigations.

Seafloor Monitoring

The Seafloor Monitoring Program in the GOM Region began in 1997 as a way to assess industry compliance with mitigations applied to offshore activities, which typically consist of avoidance criteria of seafloor features. The Seafloor Monitoring Program is comprised of a pool of scientific divers from MMS that, since its inception, has ranged in number from five to eight members. At present, the team consists of three biologists, two archaeologists, and one geophysicist. In addition to the divers, the team has one non-diving, sidescan-sonar operator who is also an archaeologist. In addition to monitoring industry compliance with environmental mitigations, the Seafloor Monitoring Team also supports the MMS Environmental Studies Program by conducting contract inspections and oversight of fieldwork.

Over the last 10 years (1997 through 2006), the Seafloor Monitoring Team has completed 53 field investigations to verify archaeological and biological mitigations, to inspect industry activity on pipeline and well-site construction, and to support the MMS Environmental Studies Program.

Long-term Monitoring at the Flower Garden Banks National Marine Sanctuary

Following the designation of the Flower Garden Banks as a National Marine Sanctuary in 1992, MMS, in consultation with academia and industry, implemented a program to monitor changes in coral populations and growth, as well as explore other important factors associated with these reefs. These monitoring studies have demonstrated that the shunting requirements of the Topographic Features Stipulation are effective in preventing the muds and cuttings from impacting the biota of the banks. Through establishment of the Flower Garden Banks National Marine Sanctuary, MMS made substantial progress in implementing many of the recommendations of previous monitoring reports.

During the 1998-2001 period, analysis of monitoring data indicated that the Flower Garden Banks were healthy and productive (Dokken et al., 2003). This monitoring effort was designed to assess the health of the coral reefs, evaluate changes in coral population levels, measure coral and algae cover and growth rates, and investigate other community characteristics. The goal of the program is to address concerns related to both gradual and punctuated degradation of these unique offshore ecosystems. Such data are useful in assessing the impacts of industrial activities, as well as their value to resource management. No significant impact from oil/gas production activity has been documented after Sanctuary designation.

Long-term monitoring has continued on a yearly basis at both banks through an equal partnership with MMS and NMFS. This monitoring not only expands MMS's knowledge and understanding of the Flower Garden Banks ecosystem, but it also improves the foundation from which management decisions are made.

In addition, another MMS study, *Post-Hurricane Assessment of Sensitive Habitats of the Flower Garden Banks Vicinity* (Precht et al., in preparation (a)), is investigating hurricane effects at the East Flower Garden, Sonnier, McGrail, Geyer, and Bright Banks.

Inspection Program

The Outer Continental Shelf Lands Act (OCSLA) authorizes and requires MMS to provide for both an annual scheduled inspection and a periodic unscheduled (unannounced) inspection of all oil and gas operations on the OCS. The GOM Region has an extensive, detailed inspection program to ensure safe and environmentally sound offshore oil and gas operations. This program places MMS inspectors offshore on drilling rigs and production platforms on a daily basis to assure compliance with all regulatory constraints that allowed commencement of the operation.

4. IMPACT ANALYSIS

4.1. UPDATE OF PROJECTIONS OF POTENTIAL ACTIVITY FROM THE PROPOSED ACTION

In order to describe the level of activity that could reasonably result from a proposed lease sale, MMS develops exploration and development scenarios of onshore and offshore activity. These scenarios provide a framework for detailed analyses of potential environmental and socioeconomic impacts of a proposed lease sale.

4.1.1. Offshore Impact-Producing Factors and Scenario

The Multisale EIS discusses projections for activities associated with a typical proposed CPA lease sale. The estimated amounts of resources projected to be leased, discovered, developed, and produced as a result of proposed CPA Lease Sale 206 are 0.776-1.292 BBO and 3.236-5.229 Tcf of gas. **Table 1** provides a summary of the major scenario elements of proposed Lease Sale 206 and some of the related impact-producing factors by offshore subareas based upon ranges in water depth (**Figure 3**). Chapter 4.1.1 of the Multisale EIS describes the offshore infrastructure and activities (impact-producing factors) associated with the proposed lease sales and with the OCS Program that could potentially affect the biological, physical, and socioeconomic resources of the GOM.

Table 1

Offshore Scenario Information Related to Proposed Lease Sale 206

	Offshore Subareas*								
	C0-60 (western)	C0-60 (eastern)	C60-200	C200-400	C400-800	C800-1600	C1600-2400	C>2400	Total CPA**
Wells Drilled									
Exploration and Delineation Wells	14 - 16	3	9 - 12	7 - 11	9 - 14	10 - 18	7 - 12	6 - 10	65 - 96
Development Wells	51 - 59	9 - 10	22 - 26	75 - 107	61 - 83	56 - 91	37 - 59	20 - 33	330 - 468
Oil Wells	13 - 15	2 - 2	7 - 8	43 - 61	36 - 49	33 - 54	22 - 36	12 - 20	168 - 245
Gas Wells	38 - 44	7 - 8	15 - 18	32 - 46	25 - 33	23 - 37	15 - 23	8 - 14	162 - 223
Workovers and Other Well Activities	309 - 357	55 - 63	133 - 161	455 - 651	371 - 504	343 - 553	224 - 357	119 - 203	2,009 - 2,849
Production Structures									
Installed	17 - 18	3	2 - 3	1 - 3	1 - 3	1 - 4	1 - 3	2	28 - 39
Removed Using Explosives	10	2	2	0 - 1	0 - 1	0	0	0	14 - 16
Total Removed	14	2 - 3	2 - 3	1 - 3	1 - 3	1 - 4	1 - 3	2	24 - 35
Method of Oil Transportation***									
Percent Piped	99%	99%	100%	100%	100%	0% - 50%	0% - 100%	0% - 100%	57% - >99%
Percent Barged	1%	1%	0%	0%	0%	0%	0%	0%	<1%
Percent Tankered	0%	0%	0%	0%	0%	0% - 50%	0% - 100%	0% - 100%	0% - 43%
Length of Installed Pipelines (km)#	40 - 720	10 - 130	NA	NA	NA	NA	NA	NA	130 - 1,700
Blowouts	0	0	0	0	0 - 1	0 - 1	0	00	2 - 3
Service-Vessel Trips (1,000 round trips)	18 - 19	3	3 - 4	4 - 7	19 - 52	19 - 68	18 - 51	33 - 34	117 - 239
Helicopter Operations (1,000 operations)	607 - 1,016	107 - 169	71 - 169	36 - 169	36 - 169	36 - 226	36 - 169	71 - 113	1,000 - 2,200

* See Figure 3.
** Subarea totals may not add up to the planning area total because of rounding.
*** 100% of gas is assumed to be piped.
\# Projected length of OCS pipelines does not include length in State waters.
NA means that information is not available.

Figure 3.   Offshore Subareas in the Proposed Sale Area.

The analysis of potential environmental and socioeconomic impacts presented in past EIS's and EA's were based on these exploration and development activity scenarios that, in most cases, were overestimated. If the level of activity was overestimated, the environmental and socioeconomic impacts of a lease sale may have been overstated. Based on a recent analysis prepared by MMS, slightly over half of the time the actual activity fell below the lowest level of forecasted activity (USDOI, MMS, 2007d). When within the forecasted range, the majority of time the actual activity was at or near the low end of the forecasted range. In addition, a single lease sale accounts for only a small percentage of the total OCS activities.

The examination of previously forecasted activity did not include the proposed lease sales addressed in the Multisale EIS. In late 2002, MMS contracted with Innovation & Information Consultants, Inc. (IIC, Inc.) to develop a model that would estimate oil and gas exploration and discovery, development, and production activity in the Gulf of Mexico. The Exploration, Development, and Production (EDP) model was delivered to MMS in 2004. The activity scenario presented in the Multisale EIS was the first developed with the EDP model. The proposed sales and their resulting activity had not yet taken place and, therefore, could not be included in the analysis.

Documentation of the EDP model and its subcomponents can be found in Ashton et al. (2004). As stated in the model's documentation, the EDP model "incorporates actual historical data, and allows easy comparison between the actual historical data, and the future model years." As the model was developed, modifications were made so that the model more accurately portrayed historical precedent.

The EDP model relies on more factors than previous modeling methods (Upton and Ashton, 2005). Constraints include leasing policy, rig availability, and resource assessment. Inputs include prices, costs, field characteristics, reserve growth, and policy variables. The production function is based on historical production data by field size and location. Another improvement over previously used modeling methods is that the EDP model defines undiscovered resources by field instead of a Gulfwide undiscovered resource volume.

A recently published MMS study to estimate physical and economic performance measures to characterize lease sales and development in the Gulf of Mexico can be used to further refine the scenario presented in the Multisale EIS (Iledare and Kaiser, 2007). The average lag of exploration and production from leases issued from 1983 to 1999 increased by water depth and decreased over time as shown in the Tables 2 and 3 below. Due to variation by water depth, exploration and production activity is staggered over time taking on average 1.9-4.5 years after a lease sale before exploration begins and 3.4-8.3 years before first production. Therefore if activity as the result of a lease sale is assumed to be to staggered over time, then the impacts and any strain on coastal infrastructure would also be staggered over time.

Table 2

Aggregate Average Lag in Months from Sales to First Spud for Leases Issued from 1983 to 1999

Water Depth	1983-1987	1985-1989	1990-1994	1995-1999
< 60m	29.3	27.8	25.8	22.9
60m - 200m	30.5	31.0	36.0	27.2
200m - 900m	40.4	46.4	42.9	30.0
>900m	84.9	93.3	84.2	53.6

Source: Iledare and Kaiser, 2007.

Table 3

Aggregate Average Lag in Months from Sales to First Production for Leases Issued from 1983 to 1999

Water Depth	1983-87	1985-1989	1990-1994	1995-1999
< 60m	59.0	53.2	49.5	41.1
60m - 200m	74.7	65.7	60.3	47.5
200m - 900m	128.1	123.0	70.2	54.1
>900m	180.6	176.9	105.9	99.6

Source: Iledare and Kaiser, 2007.

No new information has been found that necessitates a change to the offshore scenario presented in the Multisale EIS; therefore, the scenario still applies for proposed Lease Sale 206.

4.1.2. Coastal Impact-Producing Factors and Scenario

Chapter 4.1.2 of the Multisale EIS describes the onshore infrastructure and activities (impact-producing factors) associated with the proposed lease sales and with the OCS Program that could potentially affect the biological, physical, and socioeconomic resources of the GOM. Up to one new pipeline landfall and up to one new gas processing plant are projected as a result of an individual proposed lease sale. The MMS projected no other new coastal infrastructure as a result of a proposed lease sale.

The analyses of coastal infrastructure presented in the Multisale EIS and other previous EIS's and EA's concluded that no new solid waste facilities would be built as a result of a single lease sale or as a result of the OCS Program. Recent research further supports these past conclusions that existing solid-waste disposal infrastructure is adequate to support both existing and projected offshore oil and gas drilling and production needs (Dismukes et al., 2007).

The MMS projected the number of Federal OCS landfalls that may result from proposed lease sales in order to analyze the potential impacts to wetlands and other coastal habitats. In the Multisale EIS and other previous EIS's and EA's, MMS assumed that the majority of new Federal OCS pipelines would connect to the existing infrastructure in Federal and State waters and that very few would result in new pipeline landfalls. Therefore, MMS projected up to one pipeline landfall per lease sale; however, recent MMS analysis showed that even one landfall as a result of an individual lease sale may be unlikely (USDOI, MMS, 2007e). Although there will be some instances where new pipelines may need to be constructed, there is nothing to suggest any dramatic shifts in the trends in new Federal OCS landfalls given the current outlook for Gulf of Mexico development, particularly in coastal Louisiana (Dismukes, personal communication, 2007). While there are some opportunities for new pipeline landfalls from increased production activity, many of those will be limited due to a number of factors associated with basic pipeline economics.

Much of the coastal infrastructure presented in the Multisale EIS was from the *OCS-Related Infrastructure in the Gulf of Mexico Fact Book* (The Louis Berger Group, Inc., 2004). An update of the fact book is currently in progress. No new information has been found that necessitates a change to the onshore scenario presented in the Multisale EIS; therefore, the scenario still applies for proposed Lease Sale 206.

4.1.3. Hurricanes

Spills as the Result of Hurricanes

Chapter 4.1.3.4.4.2 of the Multisale EIS discusses the cause and volume of spills that resulted from the 2004-2005 hurricanes. Since the publication of the Multisale EIS, MMS has revised information and quantities of oil spillage resulting from damages caused by Hurricanes Katrina and Rita in 2005 (USDOI, MMS, 2007f). The following is a summary of the revisions.

As of July 2007, MMS has identified 154 spills of petroleum products of ≥ 1 barrel (bbl), totaling 17,077 bbl that were lost from platforms, rigs, and pipelines on the Federal OCS. This is up from MMS's January 2007 report that had identified 125 spills, totaling 16,302 bbl (USDOI, MMS, 2007g).

The July 2007 report also discussed spills of <1 bbl. Between October 2005 and June 2007, there were approximately 600 petroleum spills of <1 bbl on the Federal OCS related to the 2005 hurricanes reported to the National Response Center (NRC). These NRC reports totaled to <50 bbl and averaged approximately 3 gallons each in size. These spills of <1 bbl dissipate quickly due to evaporation, dispersion by the winds and currents, and dilution by the ocean waters. Three gallons of crude oil can briefly create a sheen of an acre (43,560 ft^2) or more in size on the ocean surface. These small releases generally do not cause identifiable environmental impacts out in the open ocean.

Unchanged from the earlier report, there were no accounts of environmental consequences resulting from spills from facilities:

- no spill contacts to the shoreline;
- no oiling of marine mammals, birds, or other wildlife;
- no large volumes of oil on the ocean surface to be collected or cleaned up; and
- no identified environmental impacts from any OCS spills from Hurricanes Katrina or Rita.

The final estimation of the total spillage associated with Hurricanes Katrina and Rita will not be complete until all operators have completed recovery efforts associated with the repair and/or have completed decommissioning of all the damaged structures. These activities will continue through 2007 and into 2008.

Damage to Offshore Infrastructure as the Result of Hurricanes

During the past few years, the Gulf Coast States and GOM oil and gas activities have been impacted by several major hurricanes. Chapter 3.3.5.7.3 of the Multisale EIS summarized the latest reports by MMS on the damage to the OCS-related platforms, rigs, and pipelines caused by Hurricanes Ivan, Katrina, and Rita.

In preparation for the 2007 hurricane season, MMS announced operational and administrative improvements that have been implemented to prepare oil and gas infrastructure in the GOM for the possibility of hurricanes during the 2007 season (USDOI, MMS, 2007h). Both MMS and industry had to reassess what possible weather conditions could occur with a major hurricane moving through the GOM. The reassessment was done through American Petroleum Institute (API) committees in which MMS was an active participant. The committees revised and updated the best practices and standards using the new information that had been collected following the 2005 hurricanes.

The MMS issued several NTL's in preparation of the 2007 hurricane season. These NTL's are summarized as follows:

Interim Guidelines for Moored Drilling Rig Fitness Requirements for the 2007 Hurricane Season (NTL 2007-G19)

During Hurricanes Ivan, Katrina, and Rita, there were 19 moored rigs that experienced a total failure of station-keeping ability. Additionally, there were several jack-up rigs that were unable to keep station through these storms. In response, MMS issued NTL 2007-G19, "Interim Guidelines for Moored Drilling Rig Fitness Requirements for the 2007 Hurricane Season," on May 25, 2007. The NTL provides guidance on the information that must be submitted with an Application for Permit to Drill (APD), demonstrating the fitness of any moored drilling rig to be used to conduct operations in the GOM OCS during the 2007 hurricane season. The MMS will use the recommendations in the API's newly developed *Recommended Practice 95F, 2nd Edition, Interim Guidance for Gulf of Mexico MODU Mooring Practices – 2007 Hurricane Season (API RP 95F, 2nd Edition)* (API, 2007) to guide the review and evaluation of the information and data that demonstrate the moored rig's capability to perform at the proposed location. In the NTL, MMS highly recommends operators follow the recommendations in API RP 95F, 2nd Edition as they prepare APD's to conduct drilling operations during the 2007 hurricane season.

Interim Guidelines for Tie-downs on OCS Production Platforms for the 2007 Hurricane Season (NTL 2007-G18)

During Hurricanes Ivan, Katrina, and Rita, there were six platform rigs that experienced a total failure or were significantly damaged. Additionally, there were numerous reports of platform facilities, equipment, and drilling units that were tied-down but shifted. In response, MMS issued NTL 2007-G18, "Interim Guidelines for tie-downs on OCS Production Platforms for the 2007 Hurricane Season," on May 21, 2007. The NTL provides guidance on the evaluation of tie-downs that will be used on OCS production platforms to secure drilling and workover rigs and permanent equipment and facilities during the 2007 hurricane season. As required by 30 CFR 250.900(a), operators must design, fabricate, install, use, maintain, and inspect all platforms and related structures on the OCS to ensure their structural integrity for the safe conduct of drilling, workover, and production operations, considering the specific environmental conditions at the platform location. Accordingly, MMS endorses the guidelines in API's *Bulletin 2TD, Guidelines for Tie-downs on Offshore Production Facilities for Hurricane Season, First Edition (API Bulletin 2TD)* (API, 2006) to assist in the review and evaluation of the information and data that demonstrate the ability of the tie-downs to perform during a hurricane. In the NTL, MMS highly recommends that operators follow the guidelines in API Bulletin 2TD as they prepare for operations during the 2007 hurricane season.

Hurricane and Tropical Storm Effects Reports (NTL 2007-G16)

The MMS issued NTL 2007-G16, "Hurricane and Tropical Storm Effects Reports," on May 14, 2007. The NTL provides clarification on using MMS's eWell Permitting and Reporting System to report hurricane and tropical storm effects by specifying the information included in the various hurricane and tropical storm reports, updating contact information, and updating a regulatory citation. Under 30 CFR 250.192, operators must submit statistics to MMS regarding the evacuation of personnel and the curtailment of production because of hurricanes and tropical storms. The MMS has established the Facility Shut-in Report, three facility damage reports, and the Pollution Report to supplement and provide more detail about the required evacuation and production shut-in statistics. The MMS uses these data and information to work interactively with the U.S. Coast Guard (USCG) on rescue needs and to notify the news media and interested public entities that monitor shut-in production and hurricane and tropical storm damage. The MMS uses the data from the pollution report to identify environmental and manmade assets at risk, provide background data for natural resource damage assessments, assist the USCG in prioritization and coordination of oil-spill-response operations, and for status reports to public and private entities.

Pipeline Risers Subject to the Platform Verification Program (NTL 2007-G14)

The MMS issued NTL 2007-G14, "Pipeline Risers Subject to the Platform Verification Program," on May 7, 2007. The MMS has determined that new pipeline risers are subject to a separate verification process that necessitates the use of an independent Certified Verification Agent (CVA) specifically for the pipeline riser. These pipeline risers are a critical component of any floating platform proposal and must meet stringent requirements for design, fabrication, and installation. Accordingly, MMS has developed the guidelines for the pipeline riser verification process as part of the platform verification program. The CVA responsibilities include performance of an independent stress analyses, including extreme storm response for critical design conditions.

Contact with District Offices and the Pipeline Section Outside Regular Work Hours (NTL 2007-G12)

The MMS issued NTL 2007-G12, "Contact with District Offices and the Pipeline Section Outside Regular Work Hours," on April 4, 2007. The purpose of the NTL is to describe procedures operators can use when contacting an MMS, GOM Region, District Office or the MMS, GOM Region, Pipeline Section outside of regular office hours. As required by 30 CFR 254.46(a), the National Response Center at (800) 424-8802 must immediately be notified if an offshore oil spill is observed.

4.2.   ENVIRONMENTAL AND SOCIOECONOMIC RESOURCES

A detailed impact analysis of the routine, accidental, and cumulative impacts of a typical CPA lease sale, which is representative of proposed Lease Sale 206, on environmental and socioeconomic resources can be found in Chapters 4.2.2, 4.4, and 4.5 of the Multisale EIS, respectively. The following chapters provide a summary of these potential impacts of proposed Lease Sale 206 on each environmental and socioeconomic resource and the conclusions of the analyses. The cumulative analysis considers environmental and socioeconomic impacts that may result from the incremental impact of proposed Lease Sale 206 when added to all past, present, and reasonably foreseeable future human activities, including non-OCS activities, as well as all OCS activities (OCS Program).

New information discovered since publication of the Multisale EIS is also presented below. This information was evaluated to determine if reanalysis of the impacts of proposed Lease Sale 206 was necessary. No new information was found that would necessitate a reanalysis of the impacts of proposed Lease Sale 206 upon environmental or socioeconomic resources. The analyses and potential impacts detailed in the Multisale EIS apply for proposed Lease Sale 206. New information was found that further supports or elaborates on analyses or information presented in the Multisale EIS, but it does not change the conclusions of any of the analyses in the Multisale EIS.

4.2.1.   Air Quality

The description of air quality in the Gulf of Mexico can be found in Chapter 3.1.1 of the Multisale EIS. A detailed impact analysis of the routine, accidental, and cumulative impacts of proposed Lease Sale 206 on air quality can be found in Chapters 4.2.2.1.1, 4.4.1, and 4.5.1 of the Multisale EIS, respectively. The following information is a summary of the impact analysis incorporated from the Multisale EIS.

The following routine activities associated with proposed Lease Sale 206 would potentially affect air quality: platform construction and emplacement; platform operations; drilling activities; flaring; seismic-survey and support-vessel operations; pipeline laying and burial operations; evaporation of volatile petroleum hydrocarbons during transfers and from surface oil slicks; and fugitive emissions. Supporting materials and discussions are presented in the Multisale EIS in Chapters 3.1.1 (description of the coastal air quality status of the Gulf coastal area), 4.1.1.6 (air emissions), and 4.1.1.9 (hydrogen sulfide). The parameters of this analysis are emission rates, surface winds, atmospheric stability, and the mixing height.

Emissions of pollutants into the atmosphere from the routine activities associated with proposed Lease Sale 206 are projected to have minimal impacts to onshore air quality because of the prevailing atmospheric conditions, emission heights, emission rates, and the distance of these emissions from the coastline. Impacts from proposed Lease Sale 206 activities are expected to be well within the National Ambient Air Quality Standards (NAAQS).

Portions of the Gulf Coast have ozone levels that exceed the Federal air quality standard, but the cumulative contribution from proposed Lease Sale 206 is very small. Ozone levels are on a declining trend because of air pollution control measures that have been implemented by States. This downward trend is expected to continue as a result of local as well as nationwide air pollution control efforts. Proposed Lease Sale 206 would have only a small effect on ozone levels in ozone nonattainment areas and would not interfere with the States' schedule for compliance with the NAAQS.

Accidents involving high concentrations of H_2S could result in deaths as well as environmental damage. Other emissions of pollutants into the atmosphere from accidental events as a result of proposed Lease Sale 206 are not projected to have significant impacts on onshore air quality because of the prevailing atmospheric conditions, emissions height, emission rates, and the distance of these emissions from the coastline. These emissions are not expected to have concentrations that would change onshore air quality classifications.

Emissions of pollutants into the atmosphere from the activities associated with the cumulative scenario are not projected to have significant effects on onshore air quality because of the prevailing atmospheric conditions, emission rates and heights, and the resulting pollutant concentrations. Onshore impacts on air quality from emissions from cumulative OCS activities are estimated to be within Class II PSD allowable increments.

The Offshore and Coastal Dispersion modeling results show that increases in onshore annual average concentrations of NO_x, SO_2, and PM_{10} are estimated to be less than the maximum increases allowed in the PSD Class II areas.

The modeling results indicate that all concentrations are below the maximum allowable PSD increments except 24-hr SO_2 and annual NO_2 for the Class I area. The impacts from proposed Lease Sale 206 are well within the PSD Class I allowable increment. The incremental contribution of proposed Lease Sale 206 (as analyzed in Chapter 4.2.2.1.1 in the Multisale EIS) to the cumulative impacts is not significant and is not expected to alter onshore air quality classifications.

The Gulf Coast has significant visibility impairment from anthropogenic emission sources. Area visibility is expected to improve somewhat as a result of regional and national programs to reduce emissions. The cumulative contribution to visibility impairment from proposed Lease Sale 206 is also expected to remain very small.

The conclusions above only consider the impact on air quality from OCS sources. If the onshore sources are considered, there may be considerable adverse effects on ozone concentration and on visibility (see also the Final EIS on the proposed OCS Oil and Gas Leasing Program, 2007-2012; USDOI, MMS, 2007c). Thus, the OCS contribution to the air quality problem in the coastal areas is small, but total impact from onshore and offshore emissions may be significant to the ozone nonattainment areas in southeast Texas and the parishes near Baton Rouge, Louisiana.

The MMS is responsible for assessing the potential impacts of air pollutant emissions from offshore oil and gas exploration, development, and production sources in the OCS. This responsibility is driven by the OCS Lands Act, which directs the MMS to regulate OCS emission sources to assure that they do not significantly affect onshore air quality. The MMS air quality regulations are contained in 30 CFR 250.302 through 304. In particular, MMS is responsible for determining if air pollutant emissions from oil and natural gas platforms and other sources in the Gulf of Mexico influence the ozone attainment (and nonattainment) status of onshore areas. This responsibility was mandated by the Clean Air Act Amendments of 1990 (CAAA).

In addition, the CAAA requires MMS to coordinate air pollution control activities with USEPA. Thus, there will be a continuing need for emission inventories and modeling in the future, especially with the implementation of the 8-hour ozone standard. The future area of interest is not only Louisiana and Texas but it also includes Mississippi, Alabama, and Florida. Under provisions of the CAAA, the U.S. Environmental Protection Agency's (USEPA) Administrator, in consultation with the Secretary of the Interior and the Commandant of the Coast Guard, will establish the requirements to control air pollution in OCS areas of the Pacific, Atlantic, Arctic, and eastward of 87°30'W. longitude in the Gulf of Mexico.

To assess the emissions of offshore oil and gas platforms and their associated emissions, MMS first conducted emission inventories in the GOM in the early 1990's, which was the Gulf of Mexico Air Quality Study (GMAQ) (Systems Applications International et al., 1995). To develop a base year 2000 inventory of criteria pollutant and greenhouse gas emissions for all OCS oil and gas production-related sources in the Gulf of Mexico, MMS collected activity data from platform operators during the year 2000 (Wilson et al., 2004). The 2000 emission inventory is being used until the 2005 emission inventory becomes available at the end of October 2007. Likewise, a 2008 emission inventory study has been awarded and more inventory data will be collected for 2008.

Additionally, a 5-year meteorological database will be completed soon. This database will be used by industry and MMS in point-source modeling in plans analysis to ensure there are no significant impacts to onshore areas (USDOI, MMS, in preparation).

The MMS is conducting an ongoing synthesis study (Haney and Douglas, in preparation) that will consolidate all MMS air quality studies, meteorological studies, and emissions studies into one database to determine links between parts. Also, general analysis is being done on 8-hour ozone nonattainment coastal areas and the Breton Class 1 area to ensure no there are significant impacts to onshore areas. The USEPA has proposed a new ozone 8-hour standard and they will issue final standards by March 12, 2008 (USEPA, 2007a).

The MMS is coordinating with the University of Alabama, Huntsville (UAH) on the MMS's Satellite Data Assimilation project to test a newly developed, physically consistent, method for assimilating satellite temperatures into Mesoscale Model 5 (MM5) meteorological model preprocessors. Since the MM5 meteorological model is too complex and time consuming to test software algorithms, a one-dimensional model has been developed to quickly test the new formulation and isolate the results. The UAH continues to coordinate with USEPA on the new algorithm development and model enhancements as the transition proceeds from MM5 to Weather Research and Forecast (WRF). The UAH is collaborating with NOAA/USEPA's Atmospheric Modeling Division to make this project's satellite data and assimilation techniques available to the air quality modeling community. The satellite assimilation technique will be implemented in the latest version of WRF and will likely result in meteorological improvements, which translate into air quality model improvements, resulting in better air quality model assessments of OCS impacts to adjacent onshore areas. The MMS's support of UAH research has resulted in one published technical article with two others in preparation. Likewise, MMS has operating cost on two radar wind profilers to provide additional meteorological data to use in MM5, which in return will yield a more accurate regional air quality model impacts analysis.

Figure 3-1 of the Multisale EIS presents the air quality status (i.e., ozone nonattainment) in the Gulf Coast as of September 2005. **Figure 4** below shows that the status of these coastal counties has not changed as of June 20, 2007 (USEPA, 2007b).

Figure 4.   Status of Ozone Attainment in the Coastal Counties and Parishes of the Central and Western Gulf of Mexico (USEPA, 2007b).

Air quality data for 2005 from Mississippi, Alabama, and Florida show all States in attainment of the NAAQS for all criteria pollutants (USEPA, 2005). However, Alabama's status has changed for criteria pollutant $PM_{2.5}$ Alabama has four nonattainment counties for this NAAQS (USEPA, 2007c). Jefferson, Shelby, Walker, and Jackson Counties are located in north and central Alabama; therefore, their change in status is not associated with offshore oil and gas activities or coastal infrastructure related to offshore oil and gas activity.

The MMS has reexamined the analysis for air quality presented in the Multisale EIS, based on the additional information presented above. No new significant information was discovered that would alter the impact conclusion for air quality presented in the Multisale EIS; therefore, a new analysis of the potential impacts of proposed Lease Sale 206 on air quality is not required. The analysis and potential impacts detailed in the Multisale EIS still apply for proposed Lease Sale 206.

4.2.2. Water Quality

A description of water quality in coastal and marine waters can be found in Chapter 3.1.2 of the Multisale EIS. An analysis of the routine, accidental, and cumulative impacts of proposed Lease Sale 206 on water quality can be found in Chapters 4.2.2.1.2, 4.4.2, and 4.5.2 of the Multisale EIS, respectively. The following information is a summary of the impact analysis incorporated from the Multisale EIS.

The primary impacting sources to water quality in coastal waters from routine operations are point-source and storm-water discharges from land-based support facilities, and vessel discharges while in coastal waters. The impacts to coastal water quality from proposed Lease Sale 206 should be minimal as long as all existing regulatory requirements are met.

The primary impacting sources to marine water quality during exploratory activities are discharges of drilling fluids and cuttings. During installation activities, the primary impacting sources to water quality are sediment disturbance and turbidity. Impacting discharges during production activities include produced water and supply-vessel discharges. Regulations are in place to limit the levels of contaminants in these discharges. During platform removal, sediment disturbance, gaseous by-products of explosives, or abrasive grit from cutting are the impacting discharges. Impacts to marine waters from routine activities associated with proposed Lease Sale 206 should be minimal as long as regulatory requirements are followed.

Accidental events associated with proposed Lease Sale 206 that could impact water quality include spills of oil and refined hydrocarbons, spills of chemicals or drilling fluids, and collisions and loss of well control that result in spills. Water quality is altered and degraded by oil spills through the increase of petroleum hydrocarbons and their various transformation/degradation products in the water. The extent of impact from a spill depends on the behavior and fate of oil in the water column (e.g., movement of oil and rate and nature of weathering), which, in turn, depends on oceanographic and meteorological conditions at the time. Smaller spills (<1,000 bbl) are not expected to significantly impact water quality in marine and coastal waters. Larger spills, however, could impact water quality, especially in coastal waters. Chemical spills, the accidental release of synthetic-based fluids, and blowouts are expected to have temporary localized impacts on water quality.

Coastal water quality can be cumulatively impacted by inputs, which are transported through river inflows. These inputs include hydrocarbons, trace metals, sediment, and nutrients from human activities. Cumulative impacts on the water quality of the marine environment result from the addition of discharges from exploratory and production activities to a relatively pristine environment. The incremental contribution of proposed Lease Sale 206 to the cumulative impacts on marine water quality is not expected to be significant as long as all regulations are followed.

The most recent information available was sought during the preparation of this EA for Lease Sale 206. An Internet search for relevant scientific journal articles was conducted using a publicly available search engine. In addition, the websites for Federal and State agencies, and the Gulf of Mexico Alliance were reviewed for newly released information. The Gulf of Mexico Alliance, a partnership between the Gulf States, was organized in 2005 as a collaborative means to solve regional problems to implement the U.S. Ocean Action Plan.

Although new research and ongoing monitoring information is continuously available from many sources about various water quality parameters in the Gulf of Mexico, the new information located was related to issues that have already been summarized in this EA; therefore, it was not incorporated (Ache, written communication, 2007; USEPA, 2007d-e; LADEQ, 2007a; Texas Commission on Environmental Quality, 2007).

In June 2007, USEPA issued the National Estuary Program Coastal Condition Report (USEPA, 2007f). This report was the third in a series of coastal environmental assessments. However, the first two reports covered all U.S. coastal waters, whereas this report assessed just those estuaries in the National Estuary Program. The report described conditions at four Gulf Coast estuaries near the MMS CPA and WPA, Mobile Bay, Barataria Terrebonne Estuary, Galveston Bay, and Coastal Bend Bays and Estuaries (Corpus Christi Bay Estuary). A water quality rating was determined and Coastal Bend Bays, Barataria Terrebonne Estuary, and Mobile Bay were rated fair, but Galveston Bay was rated poor due to elevated dissolved phosphorus and higher turbidity.

The USEPA's National Pollutant and Discharge Elimination System (NPDES) general permit for the Western Gulf of Mexico (GMG290000, which authorizes discharges to surface water during drilling and production) is due to expire November 5, 2007. The reissued permit is finalized and will go into effect on October 1, 2007 (USEPA, 2007g). The USEPA was a cooperating agency on the Multisale EIS, and USEPA relied on the Multisale EIS in reissuing the permit. The reissued permit will include several more stringent limitations than its predecessors. It will require submittal of the sublethal effects on growth and reproduction from the produced-water toxicity testing. It will also impose the new cooling water intake structure requirements on new offshore facilities that intake more than 2 million gallons per day, of which at least 25 percent is used for cooling purposes (Wilson, personal communication, 2007).

The zone of hypoxia on the Louisiana-Texas shelf occurs seasonally and is affected by the timing of the Mississippi and Atchafalaya Rivers' discharges carrying nutrients to the surface waters. The hypoxic conditions last until local wind-driven circulation mixes the water again. The contribution of produced water to hypoxic conditions is minimal. The amount of oxygen-demanding pollutants in produced water was determined for produced water discharged into the hypoxic zone (Veil et al., 2005) as a requirement for the reissued NPDES general permit. Existing hypoxia models were used to analyze the potential incremental impacts to the hypoxia from produced-water discharges. The USEPA determined that the potential impact of the hypoxia from produced-water discharges was insignificant (USEPA, 2007e). A large area (20,000-21,000 km^2, 7,722-8,108 mi^2) was forecasted for the 2007 hypoxic zone. This size was within 10 percent of the maximum area measured in 2002. The forecast was made in May 2007 (LUMCON, 2007a). During the mapping cruise of July 21-28, 2007, the hypoxic zone measured 20,500 km^2 (7,915 mi^2) (LUMCON, 2007b).

The MMS has reexamined the analysis for water quality presented in the Multisale EIS, based on the additional information presented above. No new significant information was discovered that would alter the impact conclusion for water quality presented in the Multisale EIS; therefore, a new analysis of the potential impacts of proposed Lease Sale 206 on water quality is not required. The analysis and potential impacts detailed in the Multisale EIS still apply for proposed Lease Sale 206.

4.2.3. Sensitive Coastal Environments

4.2.3.1. Coastal Barrier Beaches and Associated Dunes

The description, physical location, and formative processes that create the various coastal beaches and barrier island complexes are described in Chapter 3.2.1.1 of the Multisale EIS. A description of integrated shoreline environments, the barrier islands, and the dune zones that comprise and delineate the various vegetated habitats along these mainland and barrier beaches can also be found in Chapter 3.2.1.1 of the Multisale EIS. A detailed impact analysis of the routine, accidental, and cumulative impacts of proposed Lease Sale 206 on barrier islands and coastal beaches can be found in Chapters 4.2.2.1.3.1, 4.4.3.1, and 4.5.3.1 of the Multisale EIS, respectively. The following information is a summary of the impact analysis incorporated from the Multisale EIS, and this analysis addresses the impacts of proposed Lease Sale 206.

A variety of activities required to implement and support proposed Lease Sale 206 include pipeline emplacements, navigation channel use and dredging, and construction or continued use of oil and gas infrastructure. These activities are expected to be restricted to temporary and localized disturbances of the coastal barrier beaches and associated dunes. The 0-1 pipeline landfalls projected in support of proposed Lease Sale 206 are not expected to cause significant impacts to barrier beaches because of the use of non-intrusive installation methods. The projected 0-1 gas processing plants would not be expected to be constructed on barrier beaches. The use of existing facilities built inland may, through natural storm driven erosion and shoreline recession, be located in the barrier beach and dune zone and may contribute to the erosion there. Proposed Lease Sale 206 may contribute to the extended use of these facilities. No facilities are expected to be constructed on barrier beaches. Channel and inlet maintenance needed, as well as erosion protection works (jetties) required to assure access to the production and supply facilities, may contribute to minor and localized impacts on adjacent barrier beaches due to sediment deprivation. This would likely occur in the sediment starved coasts of Louisiana. Based on use, proposed Lease Sale 206 would account for a very small percentage of these impacts, which would occur whether proposed Lease Sale 206 is implemented or not. Strategic placement of dredged material from channel maintenance, channel deepening, or related actions can mitigate adverse impacts upon those localized areas. Proposed Lease Sale 206 is not expected to adversely alter barrier beach configurations significantly beyond existing, ongoing impacts in very localized areas downdrift of artificially jettied and maintained channels.

No significant impacts to the physical shape and structure of the barrier beaches are expected as a result of accidental events associated with proposed Lease Sale 206. The primary accidental impacts that may be associated with proposed Lease Sale 206 result from the probability of offshore or coastal oil spills contacting the barrier or coastal beaches. The probabilities of proposed-action-related spills occurring in OCS waters and contacting various parishes and counties are provided in Chapter 4.3.1 of the Multisale EIS. The risk of offshore spills ≥1,000 bbl occurring and contacting barrier beaches within 10 days is discussed in Chapter 4.3.1.8 of the Multisale EIS. Generally, the coastal, deltaic parishes of Louisiana have the highest risk of being contacted by an offshore spill resulting from proposed Lease Sale 206; Plaquemines Parish has the highest probability at 10-15 percent. Should a slick from such a spill make landfall, the volume of oil remaining in the slick is expected to be small. Coastal spills in offshore coastal waters or in the vicinity of Gulf tidal inlets present a greater potential risk to barrier beaches because of their close proximity. Inland spills that occur away from Gulf tidal inlets are generally not expected to significantly impact barrier beaches and dunes. The passage of two powerful hurricanes in

2005 (Katrina and Rita) resulted in changes in barrier island topography, lowering beach elevation and, therefore, potentially increasing the probability for beach oiling farther up the beach head in some locations. Due to the now more gentle slopes and, in some cases, cuts into the mainland barrier beaches left by the storms, more of the transition zone between the water and beach ridge may be more vulnerable to spills. Some areas along the Louisiana Coast, barrier islands were severely damaged either by heavily degrading beach front elevations and beach ridges, completely overtopping the islands by either removing or completely redistributing the sediments on the island so that the island becomes submerged. Should a spill contact a barrier beach, oiling is expected to be light and sand removal during cleanup activities should be minimized. No significant impacts to the physical shape and structure of barrier beaches and associated dunes are expected to occur as a result of proposed Lease Sale 206.

The already eroded Louisiana barrier island chain was damaged significantly by Hurricanes Katrina and Rita, thus further lowering the protection afforded the mainland marshes and beaches from oil spills that these barrier features previously provided. Breton Island, one of the islands comprising the hard-hit Chandeleur barrier island chain, lost approximately 50 percent of its land mass (Hall, 2006).

Under the cumulative scenario, river channelization, sediment deprivation, tropical and extra-tropical storm activity, sea-level rise, and rapid submergence will continue to result in severe, rapid erosion of most shoreline landforms along the Louisiana coast. The barrier system of coastal Mississippi and Alabama is well supported on a coastal barrier platform of sand. The Texas coast has experienced landloss because of a decrease in the volume of sediment delivered to the coast because of dams on coastal rivers, a natural decrease in sediment supply as a result of climatic changes during the past several thousand years, and subsidence along the coast. Louisiana is currently continuing to initiate ongoing, State- and federally-sponsored coastal programs and projects through the Coastal Wetlands, Planning, Protection and Restoration Act (CWPPRA) and Louisiana Coastal Area (LCA) programs, along with the federally-funded Coastal Impact Assistance Program (CIAP) initiatives being finalized and managed by MMS. All of these programs will cumulatively protect, build, restore, and enhance coastal ecosystems, and they will attempt to reduce coastal landloss in general and will include assistance in coastal and barrier beach rehabilitation or restoration. Beach stabilization projects are considered by coastal geomorphologists and engineers to accelerate coastal erosion. Beneficial use of maintenance dredged materials could be required to mitigate some of these impacts. The impacts of oil spills from both OCS and non-OCS sources to the sand-starved Louisiana coast should not result in long-term alteration of landform if the beaches are cleaned using techniques that do not significantly remove sand from the beach or dunes. The barrier beaches of deltaic Louisiana, the Chenier Plain, and the region around Galveston, Texas, have the greatest risks of sustaining impacts from oil-spill landfalls because of their very high concentrations of oil production within 50 km (31 mi) of those coasts. The cleanup impacts of these spills could result in short-term (up to 2 years) adjustments in beach profiles and configurations as a result of sand removal and disturbance during cleanup operations. Some contact to lower areas of sand dunes is expected. These contacts would not result in significant destabilization of the dunes. The long-term stressors to barrier beach communities caused by the physical effects and chemical toxicity of an oil spill may lead to decreased primary production, plant dieback, and hence further erosion. Under the cumulative scenario, new OCS-related and non-OCS pipeline landfalls are projected. These pipelines are expected to be installed using modern techniques, which cause little to no impacts to the barrier islands and beaches. Existing pipelines, in particular those parallel and landward of beaches and placed on barrier islands using older techniques that left canals or shore protection structures, have caused and will continue to cause barrier beaches to narrow and breach.

Coastal barrier beaches have experienced severe adverse cumulative impacts from natural processes and human activities. Natural processes are generally considered the major contributor to these impacts, whereas human activities cause both severe local impacts as well as the acceleration of natural processes that deteriorate coastal barriers. Human activities that have caused the greatest adverse impacts are river channelization and damming, pipeline canals, navigation channel stabilization and maintenance, and beach stabilization structures. The deterioration of Gulf barrier beaches is expected to continue in the future. Federal, State, and parish governments have made efforts over the last 10 years to slow the landward retreat of Louisiana's Gulf shorelines. Proposed Lease Sale 206 is not expected to alter adversely barrier beach configurations significantly beyond existing, ongoing impacts in very localized areas downdrift of artificially jettied and maintained channels. Proposed Lease Sale 206 may extend the life and presence of facilities in eroding areas, which would prolong erosion in those areas. Strategic placement of dredged material from channel maintenance, channel deepening, and related actions can mitigate adverse impacts upon those localized areas. Thus, the incremental contribution of proposed Lease Sale 206 to the cumulative impacts on coastal barrier beaches and dunes is expected to be very small.

A search was conducted for new information published since completion of the Multisale EIS. An electronic search of available literature and agency Internet sites, and personal interviews with various Federal and State agency researchers and mangers responsible for these coastal resources were conducted. A summary of the information found follows.

Wetland loss researchers from the U.S. Geological Survey's (USGS) National Wetland Research Center (Barras, personal communication, 2007) and the USGS Florida Integrated Science Center (Morton, personal communication, 2007) acknowledged that, while work is either ongoing or as in Florida being integrated with the State work, no additional information is available at this time for Louisiana, Mississippi, and Alabama.

The State of Florida is trying to standardize all of the different types of landloss data from various agencies and compile it into a homogenous database. Storm damage from Hurricanes Katrina and Rita did not significantly affect barrier island structure in Florida, and the damage incurred did not significantly lessen the protection of wetlands or mainland beaches (Morton, personal communication, 2007). Hurricane Ivan (2004) did the most damage to the barrier islands in Florida, and the only significant damage since then was on the east coast of Florida by Hurricane Andrea (Clark, personal communication, 2007; and Morton, personal communication, 2007). The Florida Department of Environmental Protection, Bureau of Beaches (Clark, personal communication, 2007) released a post-storm report for Hurricanes Dennis and Katrina, which addresses assessment of damages to beaches and structures (Clark and LaGrone, 2006). Along Florida's Gulf Coast, most northeastern barrier islands afford protection for beaches, while the extreme southern barrier islands protect significant wetland areas. Most of the wetlands bordering Florida's Gulf Coast are located in low energy zones in the southern part of the coast. This report also further refined previously acknowledged storm damage in northwest Florida from Hurricanes Katrina and Dennis. Eight northwest Florida coastal counties with beaches fronting on the GOM sustained significant beach erosion during the 2005 hurricane season. Three hurricanes in 2005—Dennis (July 10), Katrina (August 25), and Rita (September 20)—caused erosion and flooding along the coastal beaches of Escambia, Santa Rosa, Okaloosa, Walton, Bay, Gulf, Franklin, and Wakulla Counties. Only minor beach and dune erosion was noted in the Walton County area. The only additional damage resulting to dunes and bluffs associated with Hurricane Katrina was the further destabilization or collapse of dune systems that had been previously destabilized by Hurricane Dennis. However, following Hurricane Katrina, sedimentation closed many coastal inlets to coastal lakes, bays, and in some cases, inlets or channels associated with shipping access such as the St. Andrews Inlet near Panama City Florida.

The Texas Bureau of Economic Geology confirmed no further studies had been initiated by the State of Texas post-Rita (Tremplay, personal communication, 2007). Prior to Hurricane Rita, the Texas Bureau of Economic Geology had conducted a series of studies on the barrier islands, which is comprised of five different reports. The bureau is currently preparing a report on the Upper Strand Plain near Clam Lake and Padre Island. These studies are in the formative stages and drafts have not been released. Aerial photography of the flooded Texas coastal area following Hurricane Rita was examined, and previously flooded sites were visited post-Rita. Based on these observations, the majority of the flooded marshes are naturally reestablishing themselves and the sediment distribution along the barrier island fringe seems to appear stable.

In addition, various Internet sources were examined or revisited to determine any new information regarding barrier islands (FDEP, 2005 and 2007; Leadon, 2004; TGLO, 2007; USDOI, GS, 2006 and 2007a; White et al., 2005 and 2007). No new information was discovered from these information sources.

The MMS has reexamined the analysis for coastal beaches and barrier island complexes presented in the Multisale EIS, based on the additional information presented above. While there was some refinement of post-storm data and working drafts of various storm impacts, no new significant information was discovered that would alter the impact conclusion for coastal beaches and barrier island complexes presented in the Multisale EIS; therefore, a new analysis of the potential impacts of proposed

Lease Sale 206 on coastal beaches and barrier island complexes is not required. The analysis and potential impacts detailed in the Multisale EIS still apply for proposed Lease Sale 206.

4.2.3.2. Wetlands

A detailed description of coastal wetlands can be found in Chapter 3.2.1.2 of the Multisale EIS. A detailed impact analysis of the routine, accidental, and cumulative impacts of proposed Lease Sale 206 on coastal wetlands can be found in Chapters 4.2.2.1.3.2, 4.4.3.2, and 4.5.3.2 of the Multisale EIS, respectively. The following information is a summary of the impact analysis incorporated from the Multisale EIS. A detailed explanation of the routine and accidental impact-producing factors can be found in Chapters 4.1 and 4.3 of the Multisale EIS, respectively.

The primary impacts resulting from routine activities associated with proposed Lease Sale 206 that could affect wetlands and marshes include pipeline emplacement, construction and maintenance, navigation channel use (vessel traffic), maintenance dredging, disposal of OCS-related wastes, and the use and construction of support infrastructure in these coastal areas. Other potential impacts that are indirectly associated with OCS oil and gas activities are wake erosion resulting from navigational traffic, levee construction that prevents necessary sedimentary processes, saltwater intrusion that changes the hydrology leading to unfavorable conditions for wetland vegetation, and vulnerability to storm damage from eroded wetlands.

Wetland loss rates in coastal Louisiana are well documented to have been as high as 10,878 ha/yr (42 mi^2/yr) during the late 1960's. Studies have shown that the landloss rate in coastal Louisiana for the period 1972-1990 slowed to between an estimated 6,475 ha/yr (25 mi^2/yr) (Louisiana Coastal Wetlands Conservation and Restoration Task Force, 1993) and 9,072 ha/yr (35 mi^2/yr) (USDOI, GS, 1988). It was estimated in 2000 that coastal Louisiana would continue to lose land at a rate of approximately 2,672 ha/yr (10 mi^2/yr) over the next 50 years. Further, it was estimated that an additional net loss of 132,794 ha (512 mi^2) may occur by 2050, which is almost 10 percent of Louisiana's remaining coastal wetlands (Barras et al., 2003). However, in 2005 Hurricanes Katrina and Rita caused 217 mi^2 (562 km^2) of land change, primarily wetlands to open water (Barras, 2006).

Based on the analysis of the latest satellite imagery (Barras, 2007; Barras, in press), approximately 82 mi^2 (212 km^2) of new water areas were in areas primarily impacted by Hurricane Katrina (Mississippi River Delta Basin, Breton Sound Basin, Pontchartrain Basin, and Pearl River Basin), whereas 99 mi^2 (256 km^2) were in areas primarily impacted by Hurricane Rita (Calcasieu/Sabine Basin, Mermentau Basin, Teche/Vermilion Basin, Atchafalaya Basin, and Terrebonne Basin). Barataria Basin contained new water areas caused by both hurricanes, resulting in some 18 mi^2 (46.6 km^2) of new water areas. The fresh marsh and intermediate marsh communities' land areas decreased by 122 mi^2 (316 km^2) and 90 mi^2 (233.1 km^2), respectively, and the brackish marsh and saline marsh communities' land areas decreased by 33 mi^2 (85.5 km^2) and 28 mi^2 (72.5 km^2), respectively. These new water areas represent landlosses caused by the direct removal of wetlands. These areas also indicate transitory changes in water area caused by remnant flooding, removal of aquatic vegetation, scouring of marsh vegetation, and water-level variation attributed to normal tidal and meteorological variation between satellite images. Barras (2007) noted permanent losses cannot be estimated until several growing seasons have passed and the transitory impacts of the hurricanes are minimized. It is, however, too early to estimate the actual overall marsh loss.

The cumulative effects of human and natural activities in the coastal area have severely degraded the deltaic processes and shifted the coastal area from a condition of net land building to one of net landloss (USACOE, 2004).

Effects of routine activities to coastal wetlands associated with proposed Lease Sale 206 are expected to be low. The loss of 0-8 ha (0-20 ac) of wetlands habitat is estimated as a result of 0-2 km (0-1.2 mi) of new onshore pipelines projected as a result of proposed Lease Sale 206. Maintenance dredging of navigation channels and canals is expected to occur with minimal impacts; proposed Lease Sale 206 is expected to contribute minimally to the need for this dredging. Alternative, dredged-material disposal methods can be used to enhance and create coastal wetlands. Vessel traffic associated with a proposed action is expected to contribute minimally to the erosion and widening of navigation channels and canals. The already eroded Louisiana barrier island chain was damaged significantly by Hurricanes Katrina and Rita, thus further lowering the protection afforded the mainland marshes and beaches from oil spills that these barrier features previously provided. Breton Island, one of the islands comprising the hard-hit Chandeleur barrier island chain, lost approximately 50 percent of its landmass (Hall, 2006). Overall, impacts from these sources are expected to be low and could be further reduced through mitigation, such as horizontal, directional (trenchless) drilling techniques to avoid damages to these sensitive habitats. Secondary impacts to wetlands would be primarily from vessel traffic corridors and will continue to cause approximately 0.91-1.46 ha (2.25-3.61 ac) of landloss per year.

The primary concern for potential impact from accidental activities associated with proposed Lease Sale 206 is related to oil spills. While there is a concern for offshore oil spills resulting from proposed Lease Sale 206, they are not expected to damage significantly any wetlands along the Gulf Coast. However, if an inland oil spill related to proposed Lease Sale 206 occurs, some impact to wetland habitat would be expected. Although the impact may occur generally over coastal regions, the impact has the highest probability of occurring in and around Plaquemines and St. Bernard Parishes, Louisiana. Impacts to wetland habitats from an oil spill associated with activities related to proposed Lease Sale 206 would be expected to be low and temporary. Although the probability of occurrence is low, the greatest threat to wetland habitat is from an inland spill resulting from a vessel accident or pipeline rupture. While a resulting slick may cause minor impacts to wetland habitat and surrounding seagrass communities, the equipment and personnel used to clean up a slick over the impacted area may generate the greatest impacts to the area. Associated foot traffic may work oil farther into the sediment than would otherwise occur. Close monitoring and restrictions on the use of bottom-disturbing equipment would be needed to avoid or minimize those impacts.

Concerns were raised related to the potential impact of oil spills on the marine and coastal environments, specifically regarding the potential effects of oil spills on tourism, emergency response capabilities, spill prevention, effect of winds and currents on the transport of oil spills, accidental discharges from both deepwater blowouts and pipeline ruptures, and oil spills resulting from past and future hurricanes. The fate and behavior of oil spills, availability and adequacy of oil-spill containment and cleanup technologies, oil-spill cleanup strategies, impacts of various oil-spill cleanup methods, effects of weathering on oil spills, toxicological effects of fresh and weathered oil, air pollution associated with spilled oil, and short-term and long-term impacts of oil on wetlands are additional accidental concerns. Offshore oil spills resulting from proposed Lease Sale 206 are not expected to damage significantly any wetlands along the Gulf Coast. However, if an inland oil spill related to proposed Lease Sale 206 occurs, some impact to wetland habitat would be expected.

The already eroded Louisiana barrier island chain was significantly damaged by Hurricanes Katrina and Rita, thus further lowering the protection afforded the mainland marshes and beaches from oil spills that these barrier features previously provided.

The cumulative analysis in the Multisale EIS considers the effects of impact-producing factors related to proposed Lease Sale 206, prior and future OCS sales, State oil and gas activities, other governmental and private projects and activities, and pertinent natural processes and events that may occur and adversely affect wetlands. As a result of these activities and processes, several impact-producing factors discussed in Chapter 4.5.3.2 of the Multisale EIS will contribute to impacts on wetlands and associated habitat during the life of proposed Lease Sale 206.

There is increasing new evidence of the importance of the effect of sea-level rise (or marsh subsidence) as it relates to the loss of marsh or changes in marsh types and plant diversity (Spalding and Hester, 2007). Spalding and Hester show that the very structure of coastal wetlands will likely be altered by sea-level rise, as community shifts will be governed by the responses of individual species to new environmental conditions.

The effects of pipelines, canal dredging, navigation activities, and oil spills on wetlands are described in Chapters 4.2.1.1.3.2, 4.4.3.2, and 4.5.3.2 of the Multisale EIS. Subsidence of wetlands is discussed in more detail in Chapter 4.1.3.3.1 of the Multisale EIS. Impacts from residential, commercial, and agricultural and silvicultural (forest expansion) developments are expected to continue in coastal regions around the Gulf. Existing regulations and development permitting procedures indicate that development-related wetland loss may be slowed and that very few new onshore OCS facilities, other than pipelines, will be constructed in wetlands. Impacts from State onshore oil and gas activities are expected to occur as a result of dredging for new canals, maintenance and usage of existing rig access canals and drill slips, and preparation of new well sites. Locally, subsidence may be due to the extraction of large volumes of oil and gas from subsurface reservoirs, although subsidence associated with this factor seems to have slowed greatly over the last three decades as the reservoirs are depleted. Indirect impacts from dredging new canals for State onshore oil and gas development (Chapter 4.1.3.3.3 of the Multisale EIS) and from maintenance of the existing canal network is expected to continue. Maintenance dredging of the OCS-related navigation channels displaces approximately 492,082,500 m³ (643,619,611 yd³) of sediment per 35 years, of which 10 percent is attributed to the OCS Program. Federally maintained, non-OCS-related navigation channels are estimated to account for another estimated 36,576,500 m³ (47,840,256 yd³) of dredged material. Maintenance dredging of inshore, well-access canals is estimated to result in the displacement of another 5,014,300 m³ (6,558,457 yd³) of materials. Insignificant adverse impacts upon wetlands from maintenance dredging are expected because the large majority of the material would be disposed upon existing disposal areas. Alternative, dredged-material disposal methods can be used to enhance and create coastal wetlands. Depending upon the regions and soils through which they were dredged, secondary adverse impacts of canals may be more locally significant than direct impacts. Additional wetland losses generated by the secondary impacts of saltwater intrusion, flank subsidence, freshwater-reservoir reduction, and deeper tidal penetration have not been calculated due to a lack of quantitative documentation; the MMS has initiated a study to document and develop data concerning such losses.

A variety of mitigation efforts are initiated to protect against direct and indirect wetland loss. The nonmaintenance of mitigation structures that reduce canal construction impacts can have substantial impacts upon wetlands. These localized impacts are expected to continue. Various estimates of the total, relative direct and indirect impacts of pipeline and navigation canals on wetland loss vary enormously; they range from a low of 9 percent (Britsch and Dunbar 1993) to 33 percent (Penland et al., 2001a and b) to estimates of greater than 50 percent (Turner et al., 1982; Bass and Turner, 1997; Scaife et al., 1983). A panel review of scientific evidence suggests that wetland losses directly attributable to all human activities account for less than 12 percent of the total wetland loss experienced since 1930 and approximately 29 percent of the total losses between 1955 and 1978 (Boesch et al., 1994). Of these direct losses, 33 percent are attributed to canal and spoil bank creation (10% of overall wetland loss). In Louisiana, deepening Fourchon Channel to accommodate larger, OCS-related service vessels has occurred within a saline marsh environment and will afford the opportunity for the creation of wetlands with the dredged materials. Also, deepening the Corpus Christi and Houston Ship Channels is non-OCS related and should also afford the opportunity to create wetlands with dredged material. A variety of non-OCS-related pressures are generating a need to expand ports on the Mississippi Gulf Coast.

Based on preliminary historic landloss results from the MMS/USGS National Wetlands Research Center current coastal pipeline impacts study for the Louisiana study area, the predicted landloss from the estimated 64-94 km (40-58 mi) of new OCS pipeline construction ranges from approximately 256-376 ha (633-929 ac) total over the 40-year analysis period. This estimate does not take into account the current regulatory programs, modern construction techniques and mitigations, or any new techniques that might be developed in the future. The modern construction techniques and mitigative measures result in zero (0) to negligible impacts on wetland habitats.

The current MMS/USGS pipeline study is continuing to develop models that will aid in quantifying habitat loss associated with OCS activities. Proposed Lease Sale 206 represents about 3-4 percent of the OCS impacts that will occur during the period 2007-2046. The cumulative effects of human and natural activities in the coastal area have severely degraded the deltaic processes and shifted the coastal area from a condition of net land building to one of net land loss. Deltaic Louisiana is expected to continue to experience the greatest loss of wetland habitat. Wetland loss is also expected to continue in coastal Texas, Mississippi, Alabama, and Florida, but at slower rates. The loss of 0-8 ha (0-20 ac) of wetlands habitat is estimated as a result of 0-2 km (0-1.2 mi) of new onshore pipelines projected as a result of proposed Lease Sale 206. Secondary impacts from proposed Lease Sale 206 to wetlands would be primarily from vessel traffic corridors and will continue to cause approximately 2.25-3.61 ac/yr of landloss for proposed Lease Sale 206. However, effective mitigation and construction techniques have been and would be used to prevent or minimize landloss.

In addition, the State of Louisiana has made provision for wetlands protection and restoration part of the States' plan for hurricane protection. The Louisiana State legislature established the Coastal Protection and Restoration Authority (CPRA) and charged it with coordinating the efforts of local, State, and Federal agencies to achieve long-term and comprehensive coastal protection and restoration that integrates flood control and wetland restoration. The following four objectives were defined for the plan: reduce the risk to economic assets; restore sustainability to the coastal ecosystem; maintain a diverse array of habitats for fish and wildlife; and sustain Louisiana's unique heritage and culture. The Final

Master Plan (State of Louisiana, CPRA, 2007) was submitted to the Louisiana legislature on April 30, 2007, and was approved on May 30, 2007.

A search was conducted for new information published since completion of the Multisale EIS. A search of Internet information sources (Bernier et al., 2006; Clark and LaGrone, 2006; FDEP 2005 and 2007; USDOI, GS, 2007b-e), as well as personal interviews with personnel from State and Federal resource agencies (Cahoon, personal communication, 2007), was conducted to determine availability of recent information. Various Internet sources were examined to assess recent information regarding wetland loss or potential new threats to coastal wetlands that may be pertinent to the CPA. The search revealed a recent study indicating the very structure of coastal wetlands will likely be altered by sea-level rise, as community shifts will be governed by the responses of individual species to new environmental conditions (Spalding and Hester, 2007). While this information is not new, the study did explore, through the use of controlled experiments, how the variance in flooding regime, salinities, and the particular plant species involved may evolve in different coastal environments than presently exist. Other findings related to changes in State-mandated coastal policies addressing wetland protection, restoration, preservation, and development. John Barras with the USGS Wetland Resources Center noted that, while the current wetland loss numbers cited in the Multisale EIS have not changed significantly, marsh recovery (or land gain) varies from location to location. Marsh recovery seems to be doing well in the Caernarvon area, located in St. Bernard Parish, Louisiana, where the marsh was not completely uprooted. Other areas comprised of large shallow flats are becoming vegetated with various aquatic species, but not necessarily with viable marsh. In marsh areas in the vicinity of Pearl River, where there is still active delta providing sediments, the marshes are coming back. Current over flights have revealed large scour scars caused by the hurricane surge in some marshes as a result of Hurricane Katrina (Barras, personal communication, 2007). These scars are a result of complete uprooting of the marsh vegetation and may never revegetate depending on the depth of the scar. Where root mats have not been completely removed, the marsh is recovering. The visual over flight inspection of the area south of Stennis Space Center in Mississippi revealed a great deal of marsh loss, but no quantification of this loss is available at this time.

Based on conversations with Bob Morton of the USGS Integrated Science Center in St. Petersburg, Florida, and Ralph Clark with the Florida Department of Natural Resources, Bureau of Beaches, there has been no new information released concerning wetland loss in Florida (Clark, personal communication, 2007; Morton, personal communication, 2007). Ralph indicated that the primary wetlands along the Florida Coast are located in the more stable, low-energy environments in southern Florida around the Tampa Bay area. Florida is in the process of combining, updating, and standardizing their various vegetative inventory databases, but there is no deadline for completion at this time.

The MMS has reexamined the analysis for wetlands presented in the Multisale EIS, based on the additional information presented above. No new significant information was discovered that would alter the impact conclusion for wetlands presented in the Multisale EIS; therefore, a new analysis of the potential impacts of proposed Lease Sale 206 on wetlands is not required. The analysis and potential impacts detailed in the Multisale EIS still apply for proposed Lease Sale 206.

4.2.3.3. Seagrass Communities

The description of the biology and distribution of seagrass can be found in Chapter 3.2.1.3 of the Multisale EIS. A detailed impact analysis of the routine, accidental, and cumulative impacts of proposed Lease Sale 206 on seagrass can be found in Chapters 4.2.2.1.3.3, 4.4.3.3, and 4.5.3.3 of the Multisale EIS, respectively. The following information is a summary of the impact analysis incorporated from the Multisale EIS.

The routine activities associated with proposed Lease Sale 206 that could adversely affect seagrass communities include construction of pipelines, canals, navigation channels, and shore facilities; maintenance dredging; vessel traffic (propeller scars, etc.); and oil spills, spill-response, and cleanup activities. Environmental permit requirements for locating pipelines will result in very minimal impact to seagrass if any new pipeline runs to shore due to proposed Lease Sale 206. Impacts from routine activities resulting from proposed Lease Sale 206 are expected to have negligible effects on seagrass communities.

Pipeline construction in coastal waters would temporarily elevate turbidity in nearby submerged vegetation beds, depending upon currents. If constructed, the pipeline landfall would temporarily elevate turbidity in submerged vegetation beds near the pipeline routes. The COE and State permit requirements are expected to require pipeline routes that avoid beds of high-salinity, submerged vegetation and to reduce turbidity impacts to within tolerable limits. Hence, impacts to submerged vegetation by pipeline installation are projected to be very small and short term.

After bottom sediments are disturbed by pipeline installation, they will be generally more easily suspended by storms than before the disturbance. In estuaries, this increase is not projected to be a problem. Due to tidal flushing, this increased turbidity is projected to be below significant levels.

Dredging generates the greatest overall risk to submerged vegetation, and hurricanes cause direct damage to seagrass beds, which may fail to recover in the presence of cumulative stresses. Maintenance dredging will not have a substantial impact on existing seagrass habitat given that no new channels are expected to be dredged as a result of proposed Lease Sale 206. Increased dredging is expected only in areas that do not support seagrass beds.

Vessel traffic will generally only pose a risk to seagrass when nearshore. Beds of submerged vegetation within a navigation channel's area of influence will have already adjusted their bed configurations in response to turbidity generated there. Very little, if any, damage would then occur as a result of typical channel traffic. Generally, propwash will not resuspend sediments in navigation channels beyond pre-project conditions.

Depending upon the submerged plant species involved, narrow prop scars in dense portions of the beds will take 1-7 years to recover. Scars through sparser areas will take 10 years or more to recover. The recovery period increases with the width of the scar. Extensive damage to a broad area or damage to an already stressed area may never be corrected.

Most seagrass communities are located behind barrier islands. Because of the location of most seagrass communities, inshore oil spills pose the most severe threat. Such spills may result from either vessel collisions that release fuel and lubricants or from pipelines that rupture. If an oil slick settles into a protective embayment where seagrass beds are found, shading may cause reduced chlorophyll production and thinning of leaf density. Increased water turbulence due to storms or vessel traffic can break apart the surface sheen and disperse some oil into the water column, potentially causing some dieback of leaves for one growing season. It may take as much as 5-10 years of community succession before faunal composition resembles pre-impact conditions.

A search was conducted for new information published since completion of the Multisale EIS. Various Internet sources were examined to determine any recent information regarding seagrass. Sources investigated include the USGS National Wetlands Research Center, the USGS Gulf of Mexico Integrated Science Data Information Management System, Gulf of Mexico Alliance workshops in spring of 2007, Florida Department of Environmental Protection, USEPA, and coastal universities. Other sites were found through general internet searches.

New information was discovered from these information sources. The workshops held by the Gulf of Mexico Alliance in the spring of 2007 revealed some new research and new collations of old information (May, 2007; Vittor, 2007; Hardegree, 2007). May (2007) discussed the distribution of seagrass in southeastern Mississippi waters, finding some burial of seagrass after Hurricane Katrina, seasonal fluctuation of *Ruppia maritima*, and persistent *Halodule wrightii*. Vittor (2007) discussed seagrass in Mississippi Sound and Alabama based on four aerial surveys from 1940 to 2002. His analysis showed seagrass declines of from 52 to 88 percent in these areas since 1940. Hardegree (2007) highlighted declines in seagrass in Christmas Bay and the Lower Laguna Madre. He also analyzed propeller scarring, recovery, and regulation. One new master's thesis on seagrass communities in Biloxi Marsh, Mississippi, was published. In 2006, fish communities at sites denuded of seagrass by Hurricane Katrina resembled those of sites with no seagrass before the hurricane (Maiaro, 2007).

The MMS has reexamined the analysis for seagrass presented in the Multisale EIS, based on the additional information presented above. This new information supports previous assessments. No new significant information was discovered that would alter the impact conclusion for seagrass presented in the Multisale EIS; therefore, a new analysis of the potential impacts of proposed Lease Sale 206 on seagrass is not required. The analysis and potential impacts detailed in the Multisale EIS still apply for proposed Lease Sale 206.

4.2.4.   Sensitive Offshore Benthic Resources

4.2.4.1. Continental Shelf Benthic Resources

4.2.4.1.1. Live Bottoms (Pinnacle Trend)

The description of the biology of Live Bottoms (Pinnacle Trend) can be found in Chapter 3.2.2.1.1 of the Multisale EIS. A detailed impact analysis of the routine, accidental, and cumulative impacts of proposed Lease Sale 206 on the Pinnacle Trend can be found in Chapters 4.2.2.1.4.1.1, 4.4.4.1.1, and 4.5.4.1.1 of the Multisale EIS, respectively. The following information is a summary of the impact analysis incorporated from the Multisale EIS.

Seventy blocks are within the region defined as the pinnacle trend, which contains live bottoms that may be sensitive to oil and gas activities. These blocks are located in the northeastern portion of the CPA and are located between 60- and 120-m (197- and 394-ft) water depths in the Main Pass and Viosca Knoll lease areas.

The MMS developed the Live Bottom (Pinnacle Trend) Stipulation to protect biological resources in the Pinnacle Trend in response to concerns that disturbing any of the series of topographic irregularities might adversely affect biological communities that have developed on the surfaces of the features and affect the habitat they provide for pelagic fishes. The stipulation requires avoidance of the features during the placement of oil and gas structures and the laying of pipelines. The stipulation has been adopted in CPA sales since 1990 and has been effective in protecting the features and resident biological communities from damage. The proposed Live Bottom (Pinnacle Trend) Stipulation is presented in Chapter 2.4.1.3.2 of the Multisale EIS as a potential mitigating measure for leases resulting from proposed Lease Sale 206.

Impact-producing factors resulting from routine activities of OCS oil and gas operations include physical damage, anchoring, structure emplacement and removal, pipeline emplacement, drilling discharges, discharges of produced waters, and discharges of domestic and sanitary wastes. In addition, accidental subsea oil spills or blowouts associated with OCS activities can cause damage to live bottoms. The inclusion of the Live Bottom (Pinnacle Trend) Stipulation would preclude the occurrence of physical damage and limit other impact-producing factors. Few operations exist in the region and no community-wide impacts are projected.

Non-OCS activities in the vicinity of the hard-bottom communities include recreational boating and fishing, import tankering, and natural events such as extreme weather conditions, and extreme fluctuations of environmental conditions (e.g., nutrient pulses, low dissolved oxygen levels, seawater temperature minima, and seasonal algal blooms). These activities could cause severe damage that could threaten the survival of the live/hard-bottom communities. Ships using fairways in the vicinity of the Pinnacle Trend anchor in the general area on occasion, and numerous fishermen take advantage of the relatively shallow and easily accessible resources of regional live/hard bottoms. These activities could lead to severe and permanent physical damage. During severe storms, such as hurricanes, large waves may reach deep enough to stir bottom sediments. Because of the depth of the Pinnacle Trend area, these forces are not expected to be strong enough to cause direct physical damage to organisms living on the reefs.

Impacts from blowouts, pipeline emplacement, muds and cuttings discharges, other operational discharges, and structure removals should be minimized because of the proposed Live Bottom (Pinnacle Trend) Stipulation, and the dilution of discharges and resuspended sediments in the area. Potential impacts from discharges will probably be further reduced by USEPA discharge regulations and permits restrictions. Potential impacts from oil spills ≥1,000 bbl would be restricted because of the depth of the features (>20 m (66 ft)) (if the spill occurs on the sea surface), because subsea pipeline spills are expected to rise rapidly, and because of the low prospect of pipelines being routed immediately adjacent to live/hard bottoms. The frequency of impacts to live/hard bottoms should be rare and the severity slight. Impacts from accidents involving anchor placement on live/hard bottoms could be severe in small areas (those actually crushed or subjected to abrasions).

The incremental contribution of proposed Lease Sale 206 to the cumulative impact is expected to be slight, with possible impacts from physical disturbance of the bottom, discharges of drilling muds and cuttings, other OCS discharges, structure removals, and oil spills. Negative impacts should be restricted by the implementation of the Live Bottom (Pinnacle Trend) Stipulation and site-specific stipulations, the depths of the features, and the currents in the live/hard-bottom area.

A search was conducted for new information published since completion of the Multisale EIS. Various Internet sources were examined to determine any recent information regarding the Pinnacle Trend. Sources investigated include USGS, NOAA, USEPA, and coastal universities. Other sites were found through general Internet searches.

The MMS is the lead researcher of the Pinnacle Trend, and the results of the most recent MMS-funded studies were incorporated into the Multisale EIS. Additional information was found regarding ongoing USGS studies conducted to support MMS management (Gardner et al., 2002; USDOI, GS, 2003; Weaver et al., 2001). The USGS Florida Integrated Science Center's pinnacles project works to identify patterns of demersal fish distribution, community structure, and trophic relationships associated with reef-like carbonate banks and mounds in the Pinnacle Trend area (USDOI, GS, Florida Integrated Science Center, 2003). The present research seeks to further define the basis of physical-biological coupling, aspects of community structure and function, biotope affinities, and critical habitat parameters for hard-bottom areas in the eastern Gulf of Mexico. The project applies state-of-the-art geological tools to resolve community differentiation in terms of physical geological structure (topography), detail (surface characteristics), and topographically induced current complexity, i.e., physical mechanisms driving community structure. This work enhances the understanding of the Pinnacle Trend regional ecosystem to support MMS management and decisionmaking.

The MMS has reexamined the analysis for the Pinnacle Trend presented in the Multisale EIS, based on the additional information presented above. This new information supports previous assessments. No new significant information was discovered that would alter the impact conclusion for the Pinnacle Trend presented in the Multisale EIS; therefore, a new analysis of the potential impacts of proposed Lease Sale 206 on the Pinnacle Trend is not required. The analysis and potential impacts detailed in the Multisale EIS still apply for proposed Lease Sale 206

4.2.4.1.2. Topographic Features

The description of the biology of topographic features can be found in Chapter 3.2.2.1.2 of the Multisale EIS. A detailed impact analysis of the routine, accidental, and cumulative impacts of proposed Lease Sale 206 on topographic features can be found in Chapters 4.2.2.1.4.1.2, 4.4.4.1.2, and 4.5.4.1.2 of the Multisale EIS, respectively. A description of the Topographic Features Stipulation governing oil and gas activities near these features can be found in Chapter 2.4.1.3.1 of the Multisale EIS. The following information is a summary of the impact analysis incorporated from the Multisale EIS.

Potential OCS-related impacts include the anchoring of vessels and structure emplacement, operational discharges (drilling muds and cuttings, and produced waters), blowouts, oil spills, and structure removal. Activities causing mechanical disturbance represent the greatest threat to the topographic features. This would, however, be prevented by the continued application of the Topographic Features Stipulation.

Non-OCS activities are thought to have the greatest potential of impacting the topographic features, particularly those that could mechanically disrupt the bottom (such as anchoring and treasure-hunting activities). Natural events such as hurricanes or the collapse of the tops of the topographic features (through dissolution of the underlying salt structure) could cause severe impacts. Impacts from scuba diving, fishing, ocean dumping, and discharges or spills from tankering of imported oil are likely to have little or no impact on the topographic features.

It is assumed that a resuspension of sediments or a subsurface oil spill following a blowout could reach the biota of a topographic feature. If this were to occur, the impacts would be primarily sublethal with the disruption or impairment of a few elements at the local scale, but no interference to the general system performance would occur. Oil spills can cause damage to benthic organisms when the oil contacts the organisms. In the unlikely event that oil from a subsurface spill would reach the biota of a topographic feature, the effects would be primarily sublethal for corals and much of the other fully developed biota. It is anticipated that potential recovery for such an event would occur within a period of 2 years (USDOC, NOAA, Office of Response and Restoration, 2007; Shigenaka, 2001; Rice et al., 1983). In the highly unlikely event that oil from a subsurface spill reached an area containing coral cover (e.g., Flower Garden Banks and Stetson Bank) in lethal concentrations, the impacted area would be small, but its recovery could take in excess of 10 years. However, due to the application of the proposed

Topographic Features Stipulation, blowouts would not occur in the immediate vicinity of the topographic features and associated biota. Therefore, there would be little impact on the features.

The incremental contribution of proposed Lease Sale 206 (as analyzed in Chapter 4.2.2.1.4.1.2 of the Multisale EIS) to the cumulative impact is negligible because of the implementation of the Topographic Features Stipulation, which would limit mechanical impacts and operational discharges. Furthermore, there is a low probability and low risk of accidental OCS-related events such as blowouts and oil spills occurring in the immediate vicinity of a topographic feature.

A search was conducted for new information published since completion of the Multisale EIS. Various Internet sources were examined to determine any recent information regarding topographic features. Sources investigated include USGS, NOAA, USEPA, and coastal universities. Other sites were found through general Internet searches.

One ongoing study reports some preliminary results that indicate small shifts in benthic cover including an increase in algae and decrease in sponges (Rooker et al., in preparation). They also report some shifts in fish community composition. These shifts are likely the result of impacts from Hurricane Rita in September 2005.

The MMS has conducted studies of select topographic features since Hurricane Rita. Long-term monitoring has continued on a yearly basis at the East and West Flower Garden Banks through an equal partnership between MMS and NOAA's National Marine Sanctuary program. This monitoring not only expands MMS's knowledge and understanding of the Flower Garden Banks ecosystem, but it also improves the foundation from which management decisions are made. Another MMS study, *Post-Hurricane Assessment of Sensitive Habitats of the Flower Garden Banks Vicinity* (Precht et al., in preparation (a)), is investigating hurricane effects at the East Flower Garden, Sonnier, McGrail, Geyer, and Bright Banks. Initial assessment of the East Flower Garden Bank reveals mechanical damage from Hurricane Rita and a significant bleaching event (up to 46% of corals). This was followed by an outbreak of coral disease affecting up to 8 percent of corals at the East Flower Garden Bank. These are the most severe recorded outbreaks of bleaching and disease at the Flower Garden Banks. Other preliminary results suggest little hurricane damage to McGrail, Geyer, and Bright Banks but severe damage at Sonnier Bank (Precht et al., in preparation (a)). Speculation is that Sonnier Bank was more affected because of its shallower depth and position on the east side of the storm track. It is also thought that repeated anchor damage has affected Sonnier Bank. Community recovery is expected to take at least 5 years if anchor damage is prevented. Monitoring at the Flower Garden Banks in 2006 and 2007 shows good recovery of corals with no significant deterioration of community health (Precht et al., 2006; Precht et al., in preparation (b)).

The MMS has reexamined the analysis for topographic features presented in the Multisale EIS, based on the additional information presented above. This new information illustrates the potential effects of natural events, especially the cumulative impacts of hurricanes. However, OCS-related oil and gas impacts remain unchanged and previous assessments are still accurate. No new significant information was discovered that would alter the impact conclusion for topographic features presented in the Multisale EIS; therefore, a new analysis of the potential impacts of proposed Lease Sale 206 on topographic features is not required. The analysis and potential impacts detailed in the Multisale EIS still apply for proposed Lease Sale 206.

4.2.4.2. Continental Slope and Deepwater Resources

4.2.4.2.1. Chemosynthetic Deepwater Benthic Communities

The description of the biology, life history, and distribution of chemosynthetic deepwater benthic communities can be found in Chapter 3.2.2.2.1 of the Multisale EIS. A detailed impact analysis of the routine, accidental, and cumulative impacts of proposed Lease Sale 206 on chemosynthetic communities can be found in Chapters 4.2.2.1.4.2.1, 4.4.4.2.1, and 4.5.4.2 of the Multisale EIS, respectively. The following information is a summary of the impact analysis incorporated from the Multisale EIS.

Chemosynthetic communities are susceptible to physical impacts from structure placement (including templates or subsea completions), anchoring, pipeline installation, or from a blowout depending on bottom-current conditions. The provisions of NTL 2000-G20 greatly reduce the risk of these physical impacts by requiring avoidance of potential chemosynthetic communities identified on required geophysical survey records or by requiring photodocumentation to establish the absence of chemosynthetic communities prior to approval of the structure or pipeline emplacement.

If the presence of a high-density community was missed using existing procedures, potentially severe or catastrophic impacts could occur due to raking of the sea bottom by anchors and anchor chains and partial or complete burial by muds and cuttings associated with pre-riser discharges or some types of riserless drilling. Variations in the dispersal and toxicity of synthetic-based drilling fluids may contribute to the potential areal extent of these impacts. The severity of such an impact is such that there would be incremental losses of productivity, reproduction, community relationships, and overall ecological functions of the community, and incremental damage to ecological relationships with the surrounding benthos. Impacts to chemosynthetic communities from any accidental release of oil would be a remote possibility.

Impacts to deepwater communities in the Gulf of Mexico from sources other than OCS activities are considered negligible. The incremental contribution of proposed Lease Sale 206 to the cumulative impact is expected to be slight, and to result from the effects of the possible impacts caused by physical disturbance of the seafloor and minor impacts from sediment resuspension.

Proposed Lease Sale 206 is expected to cause little damage to the ecological function or biological productivity of the widespread, low-density chemosynthetic communities. The rarer, widely scattered, high-density, Bush Hill-type chemosynthetic communities could experience very minor (if any) impacts from drilling discharges or resuspended sediments located at more than 1,500 ft (457 m) away as required by NTL 2000-G20.

A search was conducted for new information published since completion of the Multisale EIS. A search of Internet information sources (including scientific journals) as well as interviews with personnel from academic institutions and governmental resource agencies was conducted to determine the availability of new information. In addition, there is an ongoing MMS/National Oceanic and Atmospheric Administration Office of Ocean Exploration (NOAA-OE) co-sponsored research project, *Investigations of Chemosynthetic Communities on the Lower Continental Slope of the Gulf of Mexico*, specifically targeting chemosynthetic communities in the deep GOM (USDOI, MMS, 2006). This study was referenced in the Multisale EIS and is being tracked. Some new chemosynthetic communities were discovered in 2006 and 2007; however, they were located using the same criteria used during the biological review process for plans or pipeline applications to determine the proximity of areas with potential chemosynthetic communities.

The MMS has reexamined the analysis for chemosynthetic communities presented in the Multisale EIS, based on the additional information presented above. No new significant information was discovered that would alter the impact conclusion for chemosynthetic communities presented in the Multisale EIS; therefore, a new analysis of the potential impacts of proposed Lease Sale 206 on chemosynthetic communities is not required. The analysis and potential impacts detailed in the Multisale EIS still apply for proposed Lease Sale 206.

4.2.4.2.2. Nonchemosynthetic Deepwater Benthic Communities

The description of the biology, life history, and distribution of nonchemosynthetic deepwater benthic communities can be found in Chapter 3.2.2.2.2 of the Multisale EIS. A detailed impact analysis of the routine, accidental, and cumulative impacts of proposed Lease Sale 206 on nonchemosynthetic communities can be found in Chapters 4.2.2.1.4.2.2, 4.4.4.2.2, and 4.5.4.2 of the Multisale EIS, respectively. The following information is a summary of the impact analysis incorporated from the Multisale EIS.

Some impact to soft-bottom, benthic communities from drilling and production activities would occur as a result of physical impact from structure placement (including templates or subsea completions), anchoring, and installation of pipelines regardless of their locations. Megafauna and infauna communities at or below the sediment/water interface would be impacted from the muds and cuttings normally discharged at the seafloor at the start of every new well prior to riser installation. The impact from muds and cuttings discharged at the surface is expected to be low in deep water. Drilling muds would not be expected to reach the bottom in significant accumulations beyond a few hundred meters from the surface-discharge location, and cuttings would be dispersed. Even in situations where substantial burial of typical benthic infaunal communities occurred, recolonization from populations from neighboring soft-bottom substrate would be expected over a relatively short period of time for all size ranges of organisms, in a matter of days for bacteria, and probably less than 1 year for most all macrofauna species.

Deepwater coral habitats and other potential hard-bottom communities not associated with chemosynthetic communities appear to be relatively rare. These unique communities are distinctive and similar in nature to protected pinnacles and topographic features on the continental shelf. Any hard substrate communities located in deep water would be particularly sensitive to impacts from OCS activities. Impacts to these sensitive habitats could permanently prevent recolonization with similar organisms requiring hard substrate.

Accidental events resulting from proposed Lease Sale 206 are expected to cause little damage to the ecological function or biological productivity of the widespread, typical, deep-sea benthic communities. Some impact to benthic communities would occur as a result from an accidental blowout. Megafauna and infauna communities at or below the sediment/water interface would be impacted by the physical disturbance of a blowout or by burial from resuspended sediments. Even in situations where substantial burial of typical benthic communities occurred due to a blowout, recolonization from populations from neighboring substrate would be expected over a relatively short period of time for all size ranges of organisms in the same timeframes as described above.

Impacts to deepwater communities in the Gulf of Mexico from sources other than OCS activities are considered negligible. The incremental contribution of proposed Lease Sale 206 to the cumulative impact is expected to be slight, and to result from the effects of the possible impacts caused by physical disturbance of the seafloor and minor impacts from sediment resuspension.

Proposed Lease Sale 206 is expected to cause little damage to the ecological function or biological productivity of the widespread, typical soft-bottom, deep-sea benthic communities. Impacts to other hard-bottom communities are expected to be avoided as a consequence of the application of the existing NTL 2000-G20 for chemosynthetic communities. The same geophysical conditions associated with the potential presence of chemosynthetic communities also results in hard carbonate substrate that is generally avoided.

A search was conducted for new information published since completion of the Multisale EIS. A search of Internet information sources (including scientific journals) as well as interviews with personnel from academic institutions and governmental resource agencies was conducted to determine availability of new information.

Interest in deepwater corals has increased rapidly in the last decade as more coral systems are discovered worldwide and their importance in providing habitat for diverse communities is realized. The MMS recently published two studies on hard-bottom communities with an emphasis on *Lophelia* coral. The following are summaries of the results of these two studies, which will be used to develop additional studies of hard-bottom habitats in the deep Gulf of Mexico and which will also enhance the ability of MMS to protect sensitive, deepwater biological features.

The report, *Characterization of Northern Gulf of Mexico Deepwater Hard-Bottom Communities with Emphasis on Lophelia Coral* (CSA, 2007), presents the results of a study of 10 sites on the northern Gulf of Mexico continental slope consisting of hard-bottom areas that generally include dense assemblages of the coral *Lophelia pertusa*. Study elements include geological characterization; biological characterization, imaging, and sampling; water chemistry; and physical oceanography including short-term and long-term current meter deployments. This was the first comprehensive study of the distribution of *Lophelia pertusa* and its biology and ecology in the Gulf of Mexico. Results suggest that *Lophelia pertusa* plays a significant role in the ecology of hard-bottom habitats on the upper slope.

The report, *Seafloor Characteristics and Distribution Patterns of Lophelia pertusa and Other Sessile Megafauna at Two Upper-Slope Sites in the Northeastern Gulf of Mexico* (Schroeder, 2007), presents results of a study funded to document the seafloor characteristics and the distribution patterns of the deepwater coral *Lophelia pertusa* and other sessile megafauna at two sites in the Gulf of Mexico. The two sites, Viosca Knoll 826 (VK826) and Viosca Knoll 862-906 (VK862-906) are located on the upper DeSoto Slope subprovince. One of the sites, VK862-906, is in close proximity to the site reported from the 1950's field sampling by Moore and Bullis. The dominant taxa at both the VK862 and VK906 sites, in terms of numbers and biomass, are anemones. The largest megafauna observed were the antipatharians at VK862-906, with individual colonies estimated to be between 2.1 and 2.4 m (7 and 8 ft) tall. There appear to be at least four species of antipatharians, and collectively, they are the second most abundant megafauna taxa at both sites. The dominant megafauna taxon at the VK862 site is *L. pertusa*, which has successfully developed extensive assemblage complexes, comprised of large colony aggregations/thickets, at numerous locations. VK826 has the most extensive development of *L. pertusa* found in the Gulf of Mexico to date.

The report also discusses evidence of manmade disturbances. Furrows apparently produced when wire anchor cables, deployed in conjunction with oil and gas drilling operations conducted in this region, struck the bottom one or more times. When megafauna were present, moderate to severe damage to individual colonies or colony aggregations often resulted. However, there was no indication that extensive areawide destruction has occurred, even though these features are present throughout the main knoll survey area.

In addition, there is an ongoing MMS/NOAA-OE co-sponsored research project, *Investigations of Chemosynthetic Communities on the Lower Continental Slope of the Gulf of Mexico*, which also looked at other hard bottoms including nonchemosynthetic communities (USDOI, MMS, 2006). This study was referenced in the Multisale EIS and is being tracked. Some new deepwater coral communities were discovered in 2006 and 2007; however, they were located using the same criteria used during the biological review process for plans or pipeline applications to determine the proximity of areas with potential chemosynthetic communities that also incorporates hard bottom and potential deepwater coral habitats.

The MMS has reexamined the analysis for nonchemosynthetic deepwater benthic communities presented in the Multisale EIS, based on the additional information presented above. No new significant information was discovered that would alter the impact conclusion for nonchemosynthetic deepwater benthic communities presented in the Multisale EIS; therefore, a new analysis of the potential impacts of proposed Lease Sale 206 on nonchemosynthetic, deepwater benthic communities is not required. The analysis and potential impacts detailed in the Multisale EIS still apply for proposed Lease Sale 206.

4.2.5. Marine Mammals

The description of the biology, life history, and distribution of marine mammals in the Gulf of Mexico can be found in Chapter 3.2.3 of the Multisale EIS. A detailed impact analysis of the routine, accidental and cumulative impacts of proposed Lease Sale 206 on marine mammals can be found in Chapters 4.2.2.1.5, 4.4.5, and 4.5.5 of the Multisale EIS, respectively. The following information is a summary of the impact analysis incorporated from the Multisale EIS.

Potential effects on marine mammal species may occur from routine activities associated with proposed Lease Sale 206 and may be direct or indirect. The major impact-producing factors affecting marine mammals as a result of routine OCS activities include the degradation of water quality from operational discharges; noise generated by helicopters, vessels, operating platforms, and drillships; vessel traffic; explosive structure removals; seismic surveys; and marine debris from service vessels and OCS structures.

Small numbers of marine mammals could be killed or injured by a chance collision with a service vessel; however, current MMS requirements and guidelines for vessel operation in the vicinity of protected species should minimize this risk (the proposed Protected Species Lease Stipulation and NTL 2007-G04).

Marine mammal ingestion of industry-generated debris, which is accidentally released, is a concern. Sperm whales may be particularly at risk because of their suspected feeding behavior involving cruising along the bottom with their mouth open. Entanglement in debris could have serious consequences. A sperm whale could suffer diminished feeding and reproductive success, and potential injury, infection, and death from entanglement in lost packing materials or debris. Industry has made good progress in debris management on vessels and offshore structures in the last several years. The debris awareness training, instruction, and placards required by the proposed Protected Species Lease Stipulation and NTL 2007-G03 should greatly minimize the amount of debris that is accidentally lost overboard by offshore personnel.

There is no conclusive evidence whether anthropogenic noise has or has not caused long-term displacements of, or reductions in, marine mammal populations. Noise associated with proposed Lease Sale 206, including drilling noise, aircraft, and vessels, may affect marine mammals by eliciting a startle response or masking other sounds. However, many of the industry-related sounds are believed to be out of, or on the limits of, marine mammal hearing, and the sounds are also generally temporary. The continued presence of sperm whales in close proximity to some of the deepwater structures in the GOM tends to rule out concerns of permanent displacement from disturbance.

Seismic operations have the potential to harm marine mammals in close proximity to firing airgun arrays. The proposed Protected Species Lease Stipulation and several mitigation measures, including onboard observers and airgun shut-downs for whales in the exclusion zone, included in NTL 2007-G02, Implementation of Seismic Survey Mitigation Measures and Protected Species Observer Program, minimize the potential of harm from seismic operations to marine mammals.

Marine mammal death or injury is not expected from explosive structure-removal operations. Existing mitigations and those recently developed for structures placed in oceanic waters should continue to minimize adverse effects to marine mammals from these activities.

Contaminants in waste discharges and drilling muds might indirectly affect marine mammals through food-chain biomagnification. Although the scope and magnitude of such effects are not known, direct or indirect effects are not expected to be lethal.

Routine activities related to proposed Lease Sale 206, particularly when mitigated as required by MMS, are not expected to have long-term adverse effects on the size and productivity of any marine mammal species or population endemic to the northern GOM.

Accidental blowouts, oil spills, and spill-response activities potentially resulting from proposed Lease Sale 206 could impact marine mammals in the GOM. Characteristics of impacts (i.e., acute vs. chronic impacts) depend on the magnitude, frequency, location, and date of accidents; characteristics of spilled oil; spill-response capabilities and timing; and various meteorological and hydrological factors. Populations of marine mammals in the northern Gulf will be exposed to residuals of oils spilled as a result of proposed Lease Sale 206 during their lifetimes. Chronic or acute exposure may result in harassment, harm, or mortality to marine mammals occurring in the northern Gulf. Marine mammals made no apparent attempt to avoid spilled oil in some cases (Smultea and Würsig, 1995); however, marine mammals have been observed apparently detecting and avoiding slicks in other reports (Geraci and St. Aubin, 1987). Exposure to hydrocarbons persisting in the sea following the dispersal of an oil slick is likely to result in sublethal impacts (e.g., decreased health, reproductive fitness, and longevity; and increased vulnerability to disease) to marine mammals.

Activities considered under the cumulative scenario could affect protected cetaceans and sirenians. These marine mammals could be impacted by the degradation of water quality resulting from operational discharges, vessel traffic, noise generated by platforms, drillships, helicopters and vessels, seismic surveys, explosive structure removals, oil spills, oil-spill-response activities, loss of debris from service vessels and OCS structures, commercial fishing, capture and removal, and pathogens. The cumulative impact on marine mammals is expected to result in a number of chronic and sporadic sublethal effects (behavioral effects and nonfatal exposure to or intake of OCS-related contaminants or debris) that may stress and/or weaken individuals of a local group or population and predispose them to infection from natural or anthropogenic sources. Few deaths are expected from oil spills, chance collisions with OCS service vessels, ingestion of plastic material, commercial fishing, and pathogens. Oil spills of any size are estimated to be recurring events that would periodically contact marine mammals. Deaths as a result of structure removals are not expected to occur due to mitigation measures (e.g., NMFS Observer Program). Disturbance (noise from vessel traffic and drilling operations, etc.) and/or exposure to sublethal levels of toxins and anthropogenic contaminants may stress animals, weaken their immune systems, and make them more vulnerable to parasites and diseases that normally would not be fatal. The net result of any disturbance would be dependent upon the size and percentage of the population likely to be affected, the ecological importance of the disturbed area, the environmental and biological parameters that influence an animal's sensitivity to disturbance and stress, or the accommodation time in response to prolonged disturbance (Geraci and St. Aubin, 1980). Collisions between cetaceans and ships, although expected to be rare events, could cause serious injury or mortality. Natural phenomenon, such as tropical storms and hurricanes, are impossible to predict, but they will occur in the GOM. Generally, the offshore species and the offshore habitat are not expected to have been severely affected in the long term. However, species that occupy more nearshore habitats may have suffered more long-term impacts.

Effects of the incremental contribution of proposed Lease Sale 206, combined with non-OCS activities, may be deleterious to cetaceans occurring in the GOM. Biological significance of any mortality would depend, in part, on the size and reproductive rates of the affected stocks, as well as the number, age, and size of animals affected.

The ESA (16 U.S.C. 1631 *et seq.*), as amended (43 U.S.C. 1331 *et seq.*), establishes a national policy designed to protect and conserve threatened and endangered species and the ecosystems upon which they depend. The ESA is administered by FWS and NMFS. Section 7 of the ESA governs interagency cooperation and consultation. Under Section 7, MMS consults with FWS and NMFS to ensure that OCS activities under MMS jurisdiction do not jeopardize the continued existence of threatened or endangered species and/or result in adverse modification or destruction of their critical habitat.

The formal consultation with NMFS was concluded with receipt of the Biological Opinion (BO) on July 3, 2007 (USDOC, NMFS, 2007a). The BO concludes that the proposed lease sales and associated activities in the GOM in the 2007-2012 OCS Leasing Program, which includes Lease Sale 206, are not likely to jeopardize the continued existence of threatened and endangered species under NMFS jurisdiction or destroy or adversely modify designated critical habitat.

Section 7(b)(4)(c) of the ESA specifies that, in order to provide an incidental take statement for an endangered or threatened species of marine mammal, the taking must be authorized under Section 101(a)(5) of the Marine Mammal Protection Act (MMPA). Since no incidental take of listed marine mammals is expected or has been authorized under Section 101(a)(5)(A) of the MMPA and/or its 1994 amendments (see ESA Section 7(b)(4)(C)), no statement on incidental take of endangered whales is provided and no take is authorized. Nevertheless, MMS must immediately notify (within 24 hours, if communication is possible) the NMFS' Office of Protected Resources should a take of a listed marine mammal occur.

On December 26, 2002, MMS submitted a request for 5-year regulations under the MMPA for the taking, by harassment, of sperm whales incidental to the oil and gas industry's seismic surveys to discover oil and gas deposits offshore in the GOM. The NMFS published an Advance Notice of Proposed Rulemaking regarding the small take authorization on March 3, 2003 (68 FR 9991). Following issuance of such regulations under the MMPA, NMFS will amend this opinion to include any authorized incidental take of sperm whales, as may be appropriate at that time.

The NMFS believes that a small number of listed species will experience adverse effects as the result of exposure to a large oil spill or ingestion of accidentally spilled oil over the lifetime of the action. Spilled oil resulting from proposed Lease Sale 206 could take up to 11 nonlethal takes of sperm whales over the 40-year lifetime of the proposed lease sale. However, NMFS is not including an incidental take statement for the incidental take of listed species due to oil exposure. Incidental take, as defined at 50 CFR 402.02, refers only to takings that result from an otherwise lawful activity. The Clean Water Act (33 U.S.C. 1251 *et seq.*) as amended by the Oil Pollution Act of 1990 (33 U.S.C. 2701 *et seq.*) prohibits discharges of harmful quantities of oil, as defined at 40 CFR 110.3, into waters of the United States. Therefore, even though the BO considered the effects on listed species by oil spills that may result from proposed Lease Sale 206, those takings that would result from an unlawful activity (i.e., oil spills) are not specified in this Incidental Take Statement and have no protective coverage under Section 7(o)(2) of the ESA.

The following information was present in the BO, but not in the Multisale EIS. Based on NOAA surveys, opportunistic sightings, whaling catches, and stranding records, sperm whales in the GOM occur year-round. Sperm whales appear to favor water depths of about 1,000 m (3,281 ft) and appear to be concentrated in at least two geographic regions of the northern GOM: an area off the Dry Tortugas and offshore of the Mississippi River delta (Maze-Foley and Mullin, 2006); however, distribution also appears influenced by occurrence and movement of cyclonic/anticyclonic currents in the GOM.

The FWS and MMS have consulted informally per FWS guidance on proposed Lease Sale 206. As a result, there were no new mitigations or Terms and Conditions from FWS.

A recent report presents the results of a study that collected dive patterns of sperm whales in the Atlantic Ocean to compare with the dive patterns and social structure of sperm whales in the Gulf of Mexico (Palka and Johnson, 2007). The study started a baseline of line transect, photo-identification, oceanographic, and genetic data for the Atlantic sperm whale. Compared with the Delta region in the Gulf of Mexico, parts of the Atlantic Ocean may serve as a control population of sperm whales with little exposure to sounds of oil- and gas-related activities. The study found Gulf of Mexico sperm whales follow a foraging and socializing cycle similar to that seen for the North Atlantic whales, but North Atlantic sperm whales dive significantly deeper (average 934 m (3,064 ft) compared with 639 m (2,096 ft) for GOM whales) when foraging (Palka and Johnson, 2007).

The MMS has reexamined the analysis for marine mammals presented in the Multisale EIS, based on the additional information presented above. No new significant information was discovered that would alter the impact conclusion for marine mammals presented in the Multisale EIS; therefore, a new analysis of the potential impacts of proposed Lease Sale 206 on marine mammals is not required. The analysis and potential impacts detailed in the Multisale EIS still apply for proposed Lease Sale 206.

4.2.6. Sea Turtles

The description of the biology, life history, and distribution of sea turtles in the Gulf of Mexico can be found in Chapter 3.2.4 of the Multisale EIS. A detailed impact analysis of the routine, accidental, and cumulative impacts of proposed Lease Sale 206 on sea turtles can be found in Chapters 4.2.2.1.6, 4.4.6, and 4.5.6 of the Multisale EIS, respectively. The following information is a summary of the impact analysis incorporated from the Multisale EIS.

Routine activities resulting from proposed Lease Sale 206 have the potential to harm sea turtles. These animals could be impacted by the degradation of water quality resulting from operational discharges; noise generated by seismic exploration, helicopter and vessel traffic, platforms, and drillships; vessel collisions; and marine debris generated by service vessels and OCS facilities. Lethal effects are most likely to be from chance collisions with OCS service vessels and ingestion of plastic materials. Most OCS activities are expected to have sublethal effects.

Contaminants in waste discharges and drilling muds might indirectly affect sea turtles through food-chain biomagnification, but there is uncertainty concerning the possible effects. Rapid dilution of the discharges should minimize impact. Chronic sublethal effects (e.g., stress) resulting in persistent physiological or behavioral changes and/or avoidance of impacted areas from noise disturbance could cause declines in survival or fecundity and result in population declines; however, such declines are not expected. The required seismic operation mitigations, particularly clearance of the impact area of sea turtles prior to ramp-up, and the subsequent gradual ramping up of the airguns, should minimize the impact of rapid onset of, and close proximity to, very loud noise. Vessel traffic is a serious threat to sea turtles. Diligence on the part of vessel operators, as encouraged by the vessel strike mitigations, should minimize vessel/sea turtle collisions. Actual sea turtle impacts from explosive removals in recent years have been small. The updated pre- and post-detonation mitigations should ensure that injuries remain extremely rare. Greatly improved handling of waste and trash by industry, along with the annual awareness training required by the marine debris mitigations, is decreasing the plastics in the ocean and minimizing the devastating effects on sea turtles. The routine activities of proposed Lease Sale 206 are unlikely to have significant adverse effects on the size and recovery of any sea turtle species or population in the GOM.

Accidental blowouts, oil spills, and spill-response activities resulting from proposed Lease Sale 206 have the potential to impact small to large numbers of sea turtles in the GOM, depending on the magnitude and frequency of accidents, the ability to respond to accidents, the location and date of accidents, and various meteorological and hydrological factors. Populations of sea turtles in the northern Gulf could be exposed to residuals of oil accidentally spilled as a result of proposed Lease Sale 206 during their lifetimes. Chronic or acute exposure may result in the harassment, harm, or mortality to sea turtles occurring in the northern Gulf. In most foreseeable cases, exposure to hydrocarbons persisting in the sea following the dispersal of an oil slick will result in sublethal impacts (e.g., decreased health, reproductive fitness, and longevity; and increased vulnerability to disease) to sea turtles. Sea turtle hatchling exposure to, fouling by, or consumption of tarballs persisting in the sea following the dispersal of an oil slick would likely be fatal.

Activities considered under the cumulative scenario may harm sea turtles and their habitats. Those activities include structure installation, dredging, water quality and habitat degradation, OCS-related marine debris, vessel traffic, seismic surveys, explosive structure removals, oil spills, oil-spill-response activities, natural catastrophes, pollution, dredge operations, vessel collisions, commercial and recreational fishing, human consumption, beach lighting, and power plant entrainment. Sea turtles could be killed or injured by chance collision with vessels or eating marine debris, particularly plastic items. It is expected that deaths as a result of structure removals would rarely occur because of mitigation measures. The presence of, and noise produced by, service vessels and by the construction, operation, and removal of drill rigs may cause physiological stress and make animals more susceptible to disease or predation, as well as disrupt normal activities. Contaminants in waste discharges and drilling muds might indirectly affect sea turtles through food-chain biomagnification. Oil spills and oil-spill-response activities are potential threats that may be expected to cause turtle deaths. Contact with, and consumption of oil and oil-contaminated prey, may seriously impact turtles. Sea turtles have been seriously harmed by oil spills in the past. The majority of OCS activities are estimated to be sublethal (behavioral effects and nonfatal exposure to intake of OCS-related contaminants or debris). Chronic sublethal effects (e.g., stress) resulting in persistent physiological or behavioral changes and/or avoidance of impacted areas could cause declines in survival or productivity, resulting in either acute or gradual population declines. However, mitigations currently in place have, and will continue to, minimize sea turtle impacts. Natural phenomenon, such as tropical storms and hurricanes, are impossible to predict, but they will occur in the GOM. Generally, the offshore species and the offshore habitat are not expected to be severely affected in the long-term. However, species that occupy more nearshore habitats and those that use nearshore habitats (sea turtle nesting) may suffer more long-term impacts. The incremental contribution of proposed Lease Sale 206 to the numerous, cumulative impacts to sea turtles is not expected to be significant, especially due to mitigations currently in place.

The ESA (16 U.S.C. 1631 *et seq.*), as amended (43 U.S.C. 1331 *et seq.*), establishes a national policy designed to protect and conserve threatened and endangered species and the ecosystems upon which they depend. The ESA is administered by FWS and NMFS. Section 7 of the ESA governs interagency cooperation and consultation. Under Section 7, MMS consults with FWS and NMFS to ensure that OCS activities under MMS jurisdiction do not jeopardize the continued existence of threatened or endangered species and/or result in adverse modification or destruction of their critical habitat.

The formal consultation with NMFS was concluded with receipt of the BO on July 3, 2007 (USDOC, NMFS, 2007a). The BO concludes that the proposed lease sales and associated activities in the GOM in the 2007-2012 OCS Leasing Program, which includes Lease Sale 206, are not likely to jeopardize the continued existence of threatened and endangered species under NMFS jurisdiction, or destroy or adversely modify designated critical habitat. The NMFS issued an Incidental Take Statement on sea turtle species; the Statement contains reasonable and prudent measures (RPM's) with implementing terms and conditions to help minimize take.

The NMFS has determined that the following RPM's are necessary and appropriate to minimize impacts of the incidental take of sea turtles from vessel operation.

(1) The MMS must reduce the potential for sea turtles to be struck and injured by vessels operating in support of oil and gas development activities in the GOM.

(2) The MMS must require the monitoring and reporting of any sea turtles struck or observed to have sign of vessel interaction to assess the actual level of incidental take in comparison with the anticipated incidental take.

In order to be exempt from liability for take prohibited by Section 9 of the ESA, MMS must comply with the following terms and conditions, which implement the RPM's described above. These terms and conditions are nondiscretionary.

The following terms and conditions implement RPM No. 1.

(1) The MMS must implement NMFS measures to reduce the risk of accidental vessel strikes with sea turtles by use of its legal authorities to ensure implementation of, and compliance with NTL No 2007-G04.

The following terms and conditions implement RPM No. 2.

(1) The MMS must make information available to vessel operators concerning species information on sea turtles in the GOM and reporting of vessel-struck, or injured and dead animals.

(2) The MMS must ensure that all vessel-struck, or injured or dead turtles with indications of vessel interactions are reported to the Sea Turtle Stranding Network Coordinator in the nearest coastal state. Any takes of listed species shall be reported to the NMFS Southeast Regional Office within no more than 24 hours of the incident to takereport.nmfsser@noaa.gov. If an MMS action is responsible for the injured or

dead animals (e.g., because of a vessel strike), MMS shall require the responsible parties to assist the respective salvage and stranding network as appropriate. Report dead or injured protected species to your local stranding network contacts.

(3) The MMS must submit an annual report to NMFS Southeast Regional Office regarding the reports of vessel-struck sea turtles, and injured and dead sea turtles reported from oil and gas operators. Hardcopies of all annual reports will be submitted to the following address:

> Assistant Regional Administrator for Protected Resources
> National Marine Fisheries Service
> 263 13th Avenue South
> St. Petersburg, FL 33701

The NMFS expects impacts to sea turtles in the proposed lease sale area as a result of OCS oil and gas leasing activities. Based on stranding records, incidental captures during recreational and commercial fishing operations, scientific surveys, and historical data, the five species of sea turtles are known to occur in GOM waters in and around the proposed lease sale area. The vessel strike avoidance requirements (NTL 2003-G10) will appreciably reduce the numbers of sea turtles that may be incidentally taken from routine offshore vessel operations associated with proposed Lease Sale 206; however, the available information on the relationship between these species and OCS oil and gas activities indicates that sea turtles may be killed or injured by vessel strikes as a result of proposed Lease Sale 206. Therefore, pursuant to Section 7(b)(4) of the ESA, NMFS anticipates incidental take as follows:

- 119 lethal takes (2.9 individuals annually, on average) and 238 nonlethal takes (5.9 individuals annually, on average) of loggerhead sea turtles over the 40-year lifetime of proposed Lease Sale 206.

- 10 lethal takes (1 individual every 4 years, on average) and 21 nonlethal takes (1 individual every 1.9 years, on average) of leatherback sea turtles over the 40-year lifetime of proposed Lease Sale 206.

- 13 lethal takes (1 individual every 3 years, on average) and 26 nonlethal takes (1 individual every 1.5 years, on average) of Kemp's ridley sea turtles over the 40-year lifetime of proposed Lease Sale 206.

- 38 lethal takes (1 individual every 1.1 years, on average) and 76 nonlethal takes (1.9 individuals annually, on average) of green sea turtles over the 40-year lifetime of proposed Lease Sale 206.

- 1 lethal take and 1 nonlethal take of a hawksbill sea turtle over the 40-year lifetime of proposed Lease Sale 206.

If the actual incidental take exceeds this level, MMS must immediately reinitiate formal consultation.

The NMFS believes that a small number of listed species will experience adverse effects as the result of exposure to a large oil spill or ingestion of accidentally spilled oil over the lifetime of proposed Lease Sale 206. Spilled oil resulting from proposed Lease Sale 206 could take up to 42 lethal and 111 nonlethal takes of loggerheads; 2 lethal and 7 nonlethal takes of a leatherback sea turtles; 9 lethal and 16 nonlethal takes of Kemp's ridley sea turtles; and 13 lethal and 36 nonlethal take of green sea turtles over the 40-year lifetime of the proposed lease sale. However, NMFS is not including an Incidental Take Statement for the incidental take of listed species due to oil exposure. Incidental take, as defined at 50 CFR 402.02, refers only to takings that result from an otherwise lawful activity. The Clean Water Act (33 U.S.C. 1251 *et seq.*), as amended by OPA (33 U.S.C. 2701 *et seq.*), prohibits discharges of harmful quantities of oil, as defined at 40 CFR 110.3, into waters of the United States. Therefore, even though the BO considered the effects on listed species by oil spills that may result from proposed Lease Sale 206, those takings that would result from an unlawful activity (i.e., oil spills) are not specified in the Incidental Take Statement and have no protective coverage under Section 7(o)(2) of the ESA.

The FWS and MMS have consulted informally per FWS guidance on proposed Lease Sale 206. As a result, there were no new mitigations or Terms and Conditions from FWS.

The MMS has reexamined the analysis for sea turtles presented in the Multisale EIS, based on the additional information presented above. No new significant information was discovered that would alter the impact conclusion for sea turtles presented in the Multisale EIS; therefore, a new analysis of the potential impacts of proposed Lease Sale 206 on sea turtles is not required. The analysis and potential impacts detailed in the Multisale EIS still apply for proposed Lease Sale 206.

4.2.7. Alabama, Choctawhatchee, St. Andrew, and Perdido Key Beach Mice

The description of the biology, life history, and distribution of the Alabama, Choctawhatchee, St. Andrew and Perdido Key beach mice can be found in Chapter 3.2.5 of the Multisale EIS. A detailed impact analysis of the routine, accidental, and cumulative impacts of proposed Lease Sale 206 on beach mice can be found in Chapters 4.2.2.1.7, 4.4.7, and 4.5.7 of the Multisale EIS, respectively. The following information is a summary of the impact analysis incorporated from the Multisale EIS.

Impacts resulting from routine activities in the CPA on the Alabama, Choctawhatchee, St. Andrew and Perdido Key beach mice are possible but unlikely. Impacts may result from the consumption of beach trash and debris. Proposed Lease Sale 206 would deposit only a small portion of the total debris that would reach the habitat. Efforts undertaken for the removal of marine debris may temporarily scare away beach mice, destroy their food resources, or collapse the tops of their burrows.

Given the low probability of a large spill ($\geq$1,000 bbl) occurring, direct impacts of oil spills on beach mice from proposed Lease Sale 206 are highly unlikely. Oil-spill response and cleanup activities could have a significant impact to the beach mice and their habitat if not properly regulated.

Cumulative activities have a potential to harm or reduce the numbers of Alabama, Choctawhatchee, St. Andrew, and Perdido Key beach mice. Those activities include oil spills, alteration and reduction of habitat, predation and competition, and consumption of beach trash and debris. Most Multisale EIS-related spills, as well as oil spills stemming from import tankering and prior and future lease sales, are not expected to contact beach mice or their habitats. Cumulative activities posing the greatest potential harm to beach mice are non-OCS activities (i.e., beach development and coastal spills) and natural catastrophes (i.e., hurricanes) which, in combination, could potentially deplete some beach mice populations to unsustainable levels. The expected incremental contribution of proposed Lease Sale 206 to the cumulative impacts is negligible.

A search was conducted for new information published since completion of the Multisale EIS. A search of Internet bibliographic databases (Google, 2007; OCLC FirstSearch, 2007) as well as personal interviews with subject matter experts in other agencies was conducted to determine availability of recent information. Leblanc (personal communication, 2007) revealed that a population genetics study on the Alabama beach mouse was published in 2007 (Tenaglia et al., 2007). Adult males were often trapped with adult females, probably their mates in this monogamous species. These pairs were more distantly related than expected, probably because kin recognition allowed selection of unrelated mates to avoid inbreeding depression, reduced fitness of a population as a result of breeding of related individuals. As population levels have declined, inbreeding avoidance has become important to this subspecies. Subadults were often captured with related mice, suggesting that mice form sibling and adult-subadult familial bonds before final adult dispersal, which itself is a short distance. Consequences for inbreeding impacts remain to be investigated. Sneckenberger (personal communication, 2007) reported no new articles on beach mice in Florida.

The MMS has reexamined the analysis for the Alabama, Choctawhatchee, St. Andrew, and Perdido Key beach mice presented in the Multisale EIS, based on the additional information presented above. No new significant information was discovered that would alter the impact conclusion for the Alabama, Choctawhatchee, St. Andrew, and Perdido Key beach mice presented in the Multisale EIS; therefore, a new analysis of the potential impacts of proposed Lease Sale 206 on the Alabama, Choctawhatchee, St. Andrew, and Perdido Key beach mice is not required. The analysis and potential impacts detailed in the Multisale EIS still apply for proposed Lease Sale 206.

4.2.8. Coastal and Marine Birds

The description of the biology, life history, and distribution of coastal and marine birds in the Gulf of Mexico can be found in Chapter 3.2.5 of the Multisale EIS. A detailed impact analysis of the routine, accidental, and cumulative impacts of proposed Lease Sale 206 on coastal and marine birds can be found in Chapters 4.2.2.1.8, 4.4.8, and 4.5.8 of the Multisale EIS, respectively. The following information is a summary of the impact analysis incorporated from the Multisale EIS.

The majority of effects resulting from proposed Lease Sale 206 on endangered/threatened and nonendangered/nonthreatened coastal and marine birds are expected to be sublethal: behavioral effects, sublethal exposure to or intake of OCS-related contaminants or debris, temporary disturbances, and displacement of localized groups from impacted habitats. Chronic sublethal stress, however, is often undetectable in birds. As a result of stress, individuals may weaken, facilitating infection and disease; then, migratory species may not have the strength to reach their destination. Nocturnal circulation around platforms may create acute sublethal stress from energy loss and increase the risks of collision, while stopovers on platforms would reduce energy loss. No significant habitat impacts are expected to occur directly from routine activities resulting from proposed Lease Sale 206. Secondary impacts from pipeline and navigation canals to coastal habitats will occur over the long-term and may ultimately displace species from traditional sites to alternative sites.

Oil spills from proposed Lease Sale 206 pose the greatest potential direct and indirect impacts to coastal and marine birds. Birds that are heavily oiled are usually killed. If physical oiling of individuals or local groups of birds occurs, some degree of both acute and chronic physiological stress associated with direct and secondary uptake of oil would be expected. Small coastal spills, pipeline spills, and spills from accidents in navigated waterways can contact and affect the different groups of coastal and marine birds, most commonly marsh birds, waders, waterfowl, and certain shorebirds. Lightly oiled birds can sustain tissue and organ damage from oil ingested during feeding and grooming or from oil that is inhaled. Stress, trauma, and shock enhance the effects of exposure and poisoning. Low levels of oil could stress birds by interfering with food detection, feeding impulses, predator avoidance, territory definition, homing of migratory species, susceptibility to physiological disorders, disease resistance, growth rates, reproduction, and respiration. Reproductive success can be affected by the toxins in oil. Indirect effects occur by fouling of nesting habitat, and displacement of individuals, breeding pairs, or populations to less favorable habitats. Competition may displace refugee seabirds from all habitats.

New research, experience, and testing will help the efficacy of the rehabilitation of oiled birds and probably improve scare methods that will keep birds away from an oil slick. Rehabilitation can be significant to the survival of threatened and endangered bird species.

Dispersants used in spill cleanup activity can have toxic effects similar to oil on the reproductive success of coastal and marine birds. The air, vehicle, and foot traffic that takes place during shoreline cleanup activity can disturb nesting populations and degrade or destroy habitat if not properly regulated.

Activities considered under the cumulative activities scenario will detrimentally affect coastal and marine birds. It is expected that the majority of effects from the major impact-producing factors on coastal and marine birds are sublethal (behavioral effects and nonfatal exposure to or intake of OCS-related contaminants or debris) and will usually cause temporary disturbances and displacement of localized groups inshore. The net effect of habitat loss from oil spills, new construction, and maintenance and use of pipeline corridors and navigation waterways will alter species composition and reduce the overall carrying capacity of disturbed area(s) in general.

The incremental contribution of proposed Lease Sale 206 (Chapters 4.2.1.1.8, 4.2.2.1.1.10, and 4.4.10 of the Multisale EIS) to the cumulative impacts on coastal and marine birds is negligible because the effects of the most probable impacts, such as sale-related operational discharges and helicopters and service-vessel noise and traffic, are estimated to be sublethal, and some displacement of local individuals or groups may occur. It is expected that there will be little interaction between oil spills from proposed Lease Sale 206 and coastal and marine birds.

The cumulative effect of programmatic activities on coastal and marine birds is expected to result in a small but discernible decline in the numbers of birds with associated change in species composition and distribution. Some of these changes are expected to be permanent, as exemplified in historic census data, and to stem from a net decrease in preferred and/or critical habitat.

A search was conducted for new information published since completion of the Multisale EIS. A search of Internet bibliographic databases as well as personal interviews with authors of references used in the Multisale EIS was conducted to determine the availability of recent information since publication of the Multisale EIS. The Internet databases examined included Google (2007) and OCLC FirstSearch (2007). No new information was discovered from these information sources.

On June 28, 2007, FWS announced the removal of the bald eagle from the list of threatened and endangered species (USDOI, FWS, 2007a). The FWS will work with State wildlife agencies to monitor eagles for at least 5 years. The FWS can propose to relist the species if it appears that bald eagles again need the protection of the Endangered Species Act. The bald eagle will continue to be protected by the Bald and Golden Eagle Protection Act and the Migratory Bird Treaty Act. Both Federal laws prohibit "taking" – killing, selling, or otherwise harming eagles, their nests, or eggs.

Authors were contacted and interviewed to investigate any recent published data that may be available. A large study of military aircraft and the impacts of noise on birds offshore of California is in preparation, but it is not expected out soon (Bowles, personal communication, 2007). Nisbet (personal communication, 2007) knows of no new information on the impacts of human disturbance on birds since his own work in 2000. Flint (personal communication, 2007) knows of no new published information in 2006-2007 on the impacts of trash and debris on marine birds, particularly those with which she was familiar in the Pacific, including albatrosses at Midway Island. Jankowski (personal communication, 2007) suggested several articles from online bibliographic databases.

A literature search found Burger (1997), who reports that exposure to small amounts of oil may weaken birds or decrease their body weight so they live for years without problems until they face a severe environmental stress. Then, they have a higher mortality than unexposed birds. Burger (1993) notes that spill volume has little or no correlation with bird mortality. The density of seabirds in the affected area, wind conditions, wave action, and distance to the shore may have more effect. Khan and Ryan (1991) note substantial mortality in seabirds after attempts at rehabilitation. Sublethal symptoms of contamination were numerous and substantial prior to the mortality. Similarly, numerous symptoms were found in dead birds on the shore and in birds dying after rehabilitation that were affected by the *Prestige* oil spill in Spain on November 19, 2002 (Balseiro et al., 2005). Final major impacts to European shags (*Phalacrocorax aristotelis*) from the *Prestige* spill probably came in 2003 from a decimated food supply of fish (Velando et al., 2005). As oil weathered, the exposure of seabirds to oil from the *Exxon Valdez* spill shifted from direct oiling to ingestion with food (Hartung, 1995).

Parsons (1994) provides the following unique before and after data for impacts of a spill on birds. Extensive shoreline and salt marsh were oiled by a January 1990 Exxon spill in the Arthur Kill and Kill van Kull estuaries of New York Harbor. Double-crested cormorants had reached their pre-spill population growth by 1991. Productivity of herring gulls remained unchanged by the spill. Most heron populations increased after the spill. Great black-backed gulls had a loss of abundance. Snowy egrets and glossy ibis used salt marsh and mud flat habitat, some of which was oiled. Black-crowned night heron and glossy ibis had delayed nesting after the spill, and along with snowy egret showed lower reproductive success after the spill. Egg laying and hatching were generally more successful than chick-rearing, due to shortage of food fed to chicks. Waterfowl were not affected seriously, except for a short-term decline in mallards.

The piping plover (*Charadrius melodus*), listed as threatened, is a migratory shorebird that is endemic to North America. It winters on the Atlantic and Gulf Coasts from North Carolina to Mexico and in the Bahamas West Indies. Critical wintering habitat includes the land between mean lower low water and any densely vegetated habitat, which is not used by the piping plover. It has been hypothesized that specific wintering habitat, which includes coastal sand flats and mud flats in close proximity to large inlets or passes, may attract the largest concentrations of piping plovers because of a preferred prey base and/or because the substrate coloration provides protection from aerial predators due to chromatic matching, or camouflage (Nicholls and Baldassarre, 1990). This species remains in a precarious state given its low population numbers, sparse distribution, and continued threats to habitat throughout its range. About 2,299 birds were located on the U.S. wintering grounds during the 2001 census (Haig and Ferland, 2002). Although the results of the 2006 International Census have not yet been published, during that census, 226 piping plovers were counted at 26 sites along 201.7 km in Louisiana (Smith, personal communication, 2007).

The MMS has reexamined the analysis for coastal and marine birds presented in the Multisale EIS, based on the additional information presented above. No new significant information was discovered that would alter the impact conclusion for coastal and marine birds presented in the Multisale EIS; therefore, a new analysis of the potential impacts of proposed Lease Sale 206 on coastal and marine birds is not required. The analysis and potential impacts detailed in the Multisale EIS still apply for proposed Lease Sale 206.

4.2.9. Endangered and Threatened Fish

4.2.9.1. Gulf Sturgeon

The description of the biology, life history, and distribution of Gulf sturgeon can be found in Chapter 3.2.7.1 of the Multisale EIS. A detailed impact analysis of the routine, accidental, and cumulative impacts of proposed Lease Sale 206 on Gulf sturgeon can be found in Chapters 4.2.2.1.9.1, 4.4.9.1, and 4.5.9.1 of the Multisale EIS, respectively. The following information is a summary of the impact analysis incorporated from the Multisale EIS.

The NOAA Fisheries Service and FWS listed the Gulf sturgeon as a threatened species on September 30, 1991. Critical habitat was proposed June 6, 2002, in the *Federal Register* and was designated on April 18, 2003.

Potential impacts on Gulf sturgeon and the designated critical habitat may occur from drilling and produced-water discharges, degradation of estuarine and marine water quality by nonpoint runoff from estuarine OCS-related facilities, vessel traffic, explosive removal of structures, and pipeline installation. The dilution and low toxicity of this pollution is expected to result in a negligible impact on Gulf sturgeon as a result of proposed Lease Sale 206. Vessel traffic will generally only pose a risk to Gulf sturgeon when leaving and returning to port. Major navigation channels are excluded from critical habitat. The Gulf sturgeon's characteristics of bottom-feeding and general avoidance of disturbance make the probability of vessel strike extremely remote. Explosive removal of structures as a result of proposed Lease Sale 206 will occur well offshore of Gulf sturgeon critical habitat and the riverine, estuarine, and shallow Gulf habitats where sturgeon are generally located. Environmental permit requirements and recent techniques for locating pipelines will result in a very minimal impact to Gulf sturgeon critical habitat if any pipeline is installed nearshore due to proposed Lease Sale 206. Impacts from routine activities resulting from proposed Lease Sale 206 are expected to have negligible effects on Gulf sturgeon and their designated critical habitat.

The Gulf sturgeon could be impacted by oil spills resulting from proposed Lease Sale 206. Contact with spilled oil could have detrimental physiological effects. The juvenile and subadult Gulf sturgeon, at a minimum, seasonally use the nearshore coastal waters and could potentially be at risk from both coastal and offshore spills. However, several factors influence the probability of spilled oil contact with Gulf sturgeon or their critical habitat. The likelihood of spill occurrence and subsequent contact with, or impact to, Gulf sturgeon and/or designated critical habitat is extremely low.

The Gulf sturgeon and its critical habitat can be cumulatively impacted by activities such as oil spills, alteration and destruction of habitat, and commercial fishing. The effects from contact with spilled oil will be sublethal and last for less than one month. Substantial damage to Gulf sturgeon critical habitat is expected from inshore alteration activities and natural catastrophes. As a result, it is expected that the Gulf sturgeon will experience a decline in population sizes and a displacement from their current distribution that will last more than one generation. Deaths of adult sturgeon are expected to occur from commercial fishing. The incremental contribution of proposed Lease Sale 206 to the cumulative impact is negligible because the effect of contact between sale-specific oil spills and Gulf sturgeon is expected to be sublethal and last less than one month.

A search was conducted for new information published since completion of the Multisale EIS. A search of Internet information sources as well as interviews with personnel from State and Federal resource agencies was conducted to determine the availability of recent information. Various Internet sources were examined to determine any recent information regarding Gulf sturgeon (Florida Fish and Wildlife Commission, 2007; USDOI, FWS, 2007b and 2007c). No new information was discovered from these information sources.

State and Federal resource agencies were contacted and interviews conducted to investigate any recent published or unpublished data that may be available. Current information indicates that there may have been some displacement of sturgeon or possibly damage to their habitat in localized areas where the storm forces were strongest. The current sampling programs along the Gulf Coast indicate (at least anecdotally) that sturgeon are returning to the areas they occupied prior to Hurricane Katrina, which may indicate somewhat of a recovery of those areas (Paruka, personal communication, 2007). No changes in migratory patterns or blockages of migratory pathways have been noted. In general, the researchers noted that the sturgeon are normally found approximately 0.5 mi (0.8 km) from shore between the shoreline and the barrier islands with the bulk of the fish located in the CPA between Petit Bois, Dauphin, and Chandeleur Islands and from Perdido to Panama City as far as Fort Walton Beach (Slack, personal communication, 2007; Paruka, personal communication, 2007).

At present, NOAA indicates no changes in critical habitat have occurred, and they are working to develop an estimate of sturgeon habitat loss and a habitat suitability index for the species (Bolden, personal communication, 2007). They also have no data indicating that sturgeon are utilizing the deeper Gulf waters. In general, the mud substrates found in the Gulf waters do not support the appropriate benthic food source for Gulf sturgeon.

The MMS has consulted with NMFS for the proposed lease sales in the WPA and CPA of the GOM in the 2007-2012 OCS Leasing Program, including Lease Sale 206. The NMFS BO, signed on June 29, 2007, concludes that the proposed lease sales, including Lease Sale 206, and associated activities are not likely to jeopardize the continued existence of threatened and endangered species under NMFS jurisdiction or destroy or adversely modify designated critical habitat.

The MMS has reexamined the analysis for the Gulf sturgeon presented in the Multisale EIS, based on the additional information presented above. No new significant information was discovered that would alter the impact conclusion for the Gulf sturgeon presented in the Multisale EIS; therefore, a new analysis of the potential impacts of proposed Lease Sale 206 on the Gulf sturgeon is not required. The analysis and potential impacts detailed in the Multisale EIS still apply for proposed Lease Sale 206.

4.2.10. Fish Resources and Essential Fish Habitat

The description of the biology, life history, and distribution of fish resources and descriptions of essential fish habitat (EFH) can be found in Chapter 3.2.8.1 and 3.2.8.2 of the Multisale EIS, respectively. A detailed impact analysis of the routine, accidental, and cumulative impacts of proposed Lease Sale 206 on fish resources and EFH can be found in Chapters 4.2.2.1.10, 4.4.10, and 4.5.10 of the Multisale EIS, respectively. The following information is a summary of the impact analysis incorporated from the Multisale EIS.

It is expected that coastal and marine environmental degradation from proposed Lease Sale 206 would have little effect on fish resources or EFH. The impact of coastal and marine environmental degradation is expected to cause an undetectable decrease in fish resources or in EFH. Fish resources and EFH are expected to recover from more than 99 percent, but not all, of the expected coastal and marine environmental degradation. Fish populations, if left undisturbed, will regenerate in one generation, but any loss of wetlands as EFH would likely be permanent.

Routine activities such as pipeline trenching and OCS discharge of drilling muds and produced water would cause negligible impacts and would not deleteriously affect fish resources or EFH. At the expected level of impact, the resultant influence on fish resources would cause less than a 1 percent change in fish populations or EFH. As a result, there would be little disturbance to fish resources or EFH.

Accidental events resulting from oil and gas development in the proposed Lease Sale 206 area of the GOM have the potential to cause some detrimental effects on fisheries and commercial fishing practices. A subsurface blowout would have a negligible effect on GOM fish resources. If spills due to proposed Lease Sale 206 were to occur in open waters of the OCS proximate to mobile adult finfish or shellfish, the effects would likely be nonfatal and the extent of damage would be reduced due to the capability of adult fish and shellfish to avoid a spill, to metabolize hydrocarbons, and to excrete both metabolites and parent compounds (recognizing that spill impacts are substantial when contacting fish eggs and larvae). The effect of proposed Lease Sale 206-related oil spills on fish resources is expected to cause less than a 1 percent decrease in standing stocks of any population, landings, or value of those landings. Historically, there have been no oil spills of any size that have had a long-term impact on fishery populations.

Additional hard substrate habitat provided by structure installation in areas where natural hard bottom is rare will tend to increase fish populations. Removal of these structures will eliminate that habitat except when decommissioning results in platforms being utilized as artificial reef material. This practice is expected to increase over time.

Activities resulting from other OCS Program and non-OCS events in the northern GOM have the potential to cause detrimental effects on fish resources and EFH. Impact-producing factors of the cumulative scenario that are expected to substantially affect fish resources and EFH include coastal and marine environmental degradation, overfishing, and to a lesser degree, coastal petroleum spills and coastal pipeline trenching. At the estimated level of cumulative impact, from OCS Program and non-OCS events, the resultant influence on fish resources and EFH is expected to be substantial, but not easily distinguished from effects due to natural population variations.

The incremental contribution of proposed Lease Sale 206's impacts on fish resources and EFH to the cumulative impact is small. The effects of impact-producing factors (coastal and marine environmental degradation, petroleum spills, subsurface blowouts, pipeline trenching, and offshore discharges of drilling muds and produced waters) related to proposed Lease Sale 206 are expected to be negligible (resulting in less than a 1% decrease in fish populations or EFH) and almost undetectable among the other cumulative impacts. Even with consideration of an extreme year of major hurricane impacts to coastal wetlands in 2005, the cumulative impact of proposed Lease Sale 206 is expected to be negligible and undetectable.

At the expected level of impact, the resultant influence on fish populations and EFH from proposed Lease Sale 206 would be negligible and indistinguishable from variations due to natural causes; however, wetland loss could occur due to a petroleum spill contacting inland areas. Proposed Lease Sale 206 is expected to result in less than a 1 percent decrease in fish resources and/or standing stocks or in EFH. It would require one generation for fish resources to recover from 99 percent of the impacts. Recovery from the loss of wetlands habitat would probably not occur.

A search was conducted for new information published since completion of the Multisale EIS. A search of Internet information sources (including scientific journals) as well as interviews with personnel from academic institutions and governmental resource agencies was conducted to determine availability of new information. Significant informational Internet websites include those from the Gulf of Mexico Fisheries Management Council at http://www.gulfcouncil.org/ and the NMFS Southeast Region at http://sero.nmfs.noaa.gov/. Some recent reports from NOAA have further documented impacts from the 2005 hurricanes on fish and fishery habitat. One very recent example is *Report to Congress on the Impact of Hurricanes Katrina, Rita, and Wilma on Commercial and Recreational Fishery Habitat of Alabama, Florida, Louisiana, Mississippi, and Texas*, which was published in July 2007 (USDOC, NMFS, 2007b). This report confirms the substantial impacts of the 2005 hurricanes to nearshore habitats, especially oyster reefs. Offshore fisheries habitat sustained some impact, but not substantial. Similar information was also presented in the Multisale EIS.

The status of fish stocks in the Gulf of Mexico has also been tracked. A recent report to Congress (USDOC, NMFS, 2007c) concluded, "With the exception of oysters, available information indicates Gulf Coast marine resources were not significantly impacted by the 2005 hurricanes". In the most recent quarter through June 2007, there were no major changes in the fish stock sustainability index (FSSI) reported by NMFS (USDOC, NMFS, 2007c). The following are the only changes in overfished status of FSSI stocks in the Southeast Region (April 1-June 30):

- *South Atlantic Gag* is now approaching an overfished condition.
- *Dolphin* is now above 80 percent of maximum sustainable yield.
- *Gulf of Mexico Red Grouper* is now rebuilt.

The MMS has reexamined the analysis for fish resources and EFH presented in the Multisale EIS, based on the additional information presented above. No new significant information was discovered that would alter the impact conclusion for fish resources and EFH presented in the Multisale EIS; therefore, a new analysis of the potential impacts of proposed Lease Sale 206 on fish resources and EFH is not required. The analysis and potential impacts detailed in the Multisale EIS still apply for proposed Lease Sale 206.

4.2.11. Commercial Fishing

The description of commercial fishing in the proposed Lease Sale 206 area can be found in Chapter 3.3.1 of the Multisale EIS. A detailed impact analysis of the routine, accidental, and cumulative impacts of proposed Lease Sale 206 on commercial fishing can be found in Chapters 4.2.2.1.11, 4.4.10, and 4.5.11

of the Multisale EIS, respectively. The following information is a summary of the impact analysis incorporated from the Multisale EIS.

Effects on commercial fishing from activities associated with proposed Lease Sale 206 could result from the installation of production platforms, underwater OCS obstructions, production platform removals, seismic surveys, subsurface blowouts, pipeline trenching, and petroleum spills. Activities such as seismic surveys and pipeline trenching will cause negligible impacts and will not deleteriously affect commercial fishing activities. Seismic surveys are not expected to cause long-term or permanent displacement of any listed species from critical habitat/preferred habitat or to result in the destruction or adverse modification of critical habitat or essential fish habitat. Operations such as production platform emplacement, underwater OCS impediments, and explosive platform removal will cause slightly greater impacts on commercial fishing.

Commercial fishermen would actively avoid the area of a spill. Even if fish resources successfully avoid spills, tainting (oily-tasting fish), public perception of tainting, or the potential of tainting commercial catches would prevent fishermen (either voluntarily or imposed by regulation) from initiating activities in the spill area. This, in turn, could decrease landings and/or the value of catch for several months. The effect of proposed Lease Sale 206-related oil spills on fish resources and commercial fishing is expected to cause less than a 1 percent decrease in standing stocks of any population, commercial fishing efforts, landings, or value of those landings.

At the expected level of impact, the resultant influence on commercial fishing activities from proposed Lease Sale 206 would be negligible and indistinguishable from variations due to natural causes. As a result, there would be very little impact on commercial fishing. Proposed Lease Sale 206 is expected to result in less than a 1 percent change in activities, in pounds landed, or in the value of landings. It will require less than 6 months for fishing activity to recover from any impacts.

A search was conducted for new information published since completion of the Multisale EIS. A search of Internet information sources (including scientific journals) as well as interviews with personnel from academic institutions and governmental resource agencies was conducted to determine availability of new information. Some recent reports (USDOC, NMFS, 2007b and 2007c) have further documented impacts from the 2005 hurricanes on fish and fishery habitat discussed above under "Fish Resources and Essential Fish Habitat" (**Chapter 4.2.10** of this EA).

In July 2007, NMFS published a preliminary report for 2006 on U.S. commercial and recreational fisheries (USDOC, NMFS, 2007d). **Table 4** below shows the change in commercial landings from 2005 to 2006 for the Gulf of Mexico and the Gulf States. Despite Louisiana's drop in number of landings following Hurricane Katrina, Louisiana still remains the leader in Gulf landings, followed by Mississippi, Texas, Florida (West Coast), and Alabama. Kirkham (2007) states "though the migration into other state waters is not new, the post-storm NOAA statistics suggest a new trend: Fishers are taking more seafood from Louisiana waters than what is brought in to Louisiana ports" and "whether the trends will continue is up for debate. As docks, ramps, and icehouses in Louisiana come back online -- about 85 percent are back, according to a recent Wildlife and Fisheries report -- fishers will be able to bring their catch back to pre-storm ports and buyers" (Louisiana Department of Wildlife and Fisheries, 2007).

Table 4

U.S. Domestic Landings for the Gulf of Mexico and Gulf States, 2005 and 2006

	2005 (thousand pounds)	2006 (thousand pounds)	Change	2005 (thousand dollars)	2006 (thousand dollars)	Change
Gulf of Mexico	1,196,355	1,285,691	7%	620,987	662,938	7%
Florida, West Coast	70,230	68,913	-2%	132,781	194,023	46%
Alabama	24,032	34,052	42%	39,888	48,566	22%
Mississippi	167,609	221,838	32%	23,386	21,751	-7%
Louisiana	850,194	844,027	-1%	252,596	201,742	-20%
Texas	84,289	116,860	39%	172,337	196,856	14%

Source: USDOC, NMFS, 2007d.

The MMS has reexamined the analysis for commercial fishing presented in the Multisale EIS, based on the additional information presented above. No new significant information was discovered that would alter the impact conclusion for commercial fishing presented in the Multisale EIS; therefore, a new analysis of the potential impacts of proposed Lease Sale 206 on commercial fishing is not required. The analysis and potential impacts detailed in the Multisale EIS still apply for proposed Lease Sale 206.

4.2.12. Recreational Fishing

The description of the environment for recreational fishing is in Chapter 3.3.2 of the Multisale EIS. Detailed analysis of the routine, accidental, and cumulative impacts of proposed Lease Sale 206 on recreational fishing is in Chapters 4.2.2.1.12, 4.4.11, and 4.5.12, respectively. The following is a summary of the impact analysis from the Multisale EIS.

With respect to routine events, the development of oil and gas in the proposed lease sale area could attract additional recreational fishing activity to structures installed on productive leases. Each structure placed in the GOM to produce oil or gas would function as a *de facto* artificial reef, attract sport fish, and improve fishing prospects in the immediate vicinity of platforms. This impact would last for the life of the structure, i.e., until the structures are removed from the location and the marine environment. Proposed Lease Sale 206 would have a beneficial effect on offshore and deep-sea recreational fishing within developed leases accessible to fishermen. These effects would last until the production structures are removed from the marine environment. Short-term, space-use conflict could occur during the time that any pipeline is being installed. Impacts on recreational fishing because of OCS-related vessel wakes would be minor because, on average, vessel use associated with proposed Lease Sale 206 would represent less than 1 percent of total vessel use.

With respect to accidental events, the estimated number and size of potential spills associated with proposed Lease Sale 206's activities (Chapter 4.3.1.2 of the Multisale EIS) are unlikely to decrease recreational fishing activity but may divert the location or timing of a few planned fishing trips. Potential impacts on recreational fisheries due to accidental events as a result of proposed Lease Sale 206 would be minor to moderate. Based on the sizes of oil spills assumed for proposed Lease Sale 206, only localized and short-term disruption of recreational fishing activity might result (minor impact).

With respect to cumulative events, recreational fishing continues to be a popular nearshore and offshore recreational activity in the northeastern and central GOM. Concern for the sustainability of fish resources and marine recreational fishing has led to Federal legislation that established a fisheries management process that will include the identification and protection of EFH. The incremental contribution of proposed Lease Sale 206 (as analyzed in Chapter 4.2.2.1.12 in the Multisale EIS) to the cumulative impact on recreational fishing is positive, although minor due to the relatively small number of structures projected for the next 40 years. The cumulative impact of OCS and State oil and gas activities and import tanker spills would be minor. Implementation of proposed Lease Sale 206 would attract some private and charter-boat recreational fishermen farther offshore to the vicinity of the developed lease tracts in pursuit of targeted species known to be associated with petroleum structures in deep water.

A search was conducted for new information published since completion of the Multisale EIS. Research of recreational fishing revealed the following new information.

The NMFS has published the preliminary 2006 Marine Recreational Fisheries Statistics Survey (MRFSS) (USDOC, NMFS, 2007e). In 2006, 3.6 million residents participated in marine recreational fishing. All participants, including visitors, took nearly 25 million trips and caught almost 193 million fish. About 65 percent of the trips were made in west Florida, followed by 18 percent in Louisiana, almost 9 percent in Alabama, over 4 percent in Texas, and 4 percent in Mississippi. From 2005 to 2006, the number of recreational fishing trips from Mississippi decreased by 36 percent, while the number of trips from Alabama increased by 37 percent. Florida, Louisiana, and Texas saw smaller increases in the number of trips.

The MRFSS is the primary source for marine recreational fisheries data in U.S. waters. This survey combines random telephone interviews and onsite intercept surveys of anglers to estimate recreational catch and effort for inland, State, and Federal waters. In the GOM, surveys are conducted in western Florida, Alabama, Mississippi, and Louisiana. The Texas Parks and Wildlife Department conducts separate surveys. Tables 3-12, 3-13, and 3-14 of the Multisale EIS show MRFSS GOM data for 2005, while **Tables 5-7** show MRFSS GOM data for 2006 (USDOC, NMFS, 2007e).

Table 5

Top Species Commonly Caught by Recreational Fishers
in the Marine Recreational Fisheries Statistics Gulf Coast States (except Texas) (2006)

Species	Total All Fish (#)	Total All Fish (lbs)	Inland (#)	Inland (lbs)	Ocean (#)	Ocean (lbs)
Black drum	1,267,386	2,480,078	1,219,109	2,351,043	48,277	129,035
Dolphins	81,400	188,130	870		80,530	188,130
Gray snapper	2,594,974	1,381,957	2,043,579	483,753	551,395	898,204
Greater amberjack	66,394	683,364	1,850		64,544	683,364
Herrings	41,716,268	152,455	41,255,403	152,455	460,865	0
King mackerel	498,355	1,349,952	362,809	590,059	135,546	759,893
Mycteroperca groupers	644,735	231,395	603,463	110,062	41,272	121,333
Pinfishes	6,736,540	369,738	5,710,573	346,356	1,025,967	23,382
Red drum	8,596,876	13,576,884	8,116,594	12,063,913	480,282	1,512,971
Red snapper	1,586,841	1,485,529	62,979	33,287	1,523,862	1,452,242
Saltwater catfishes	8,773,173	862,261	7,673,254	742,800	1,099,919	119,461
Sand seatrout	3,457,656	1,237,721	3,337,144	1,180,793	120,512	56,928
Sheepshead	2,403,692	3,236,779	2,133,947	2,429,966	269,745	806,813
Spotted seatrout	30,439,521	15,500,347	29,925,279	15,196,037	514,242	304,310

Source: USDOC, NMFS, 2007e.

Table 6

Recreational Fishing Participation
in the Marine Recreational Fisheries Statistics Gulf Coast States (2006)

State	Participation Estimate (number of people)			
	Coastal	Non-Coastal	Out-of-State	Total
West Florida	2,083,835		1,988,445	4,072,281
Alabama	232,799	183,511	319,720	736,030
Mississippi	143,417	23,382	26,532	193,331
Louisiana	867,742	108,491	197,841	1,174,074
Gulf Total	3,327,793	315,384	2,532,538	6,175,716

Source: USDOC, NMFS, 2007e.

Table 7

Mode of Fishing in the Marine Recreational Fisheries Statistics Gulf Coast
States (except Texas) 2006

State	Area	Number of Trips	% of State Total
Alabama	Shore Ocean (≤3 mi)	836,479	39
	Shore Inland	372,368	17
	Charter Ocean (≤3 mi)	6,238	0
	Charter Ocean (>3 mi)	61,894	3
	Charter Inland	9,294	0
	Private/Rental Ocean (≤3 mi)	253,917	12
	Private/Rental Ocean (>3 mi)	184,991	9
	Private/Rental Inland	418,244	20
	Total	2,143,425	
West Florida	Shore Ocean (≤3 mi)	3,542,065	22
	Shore Inland	3,195,967	19
	Charter Ocean (≤3 mi)	172,528	1
	Charter Ocean (>3 mi)	268,956	2
	Charter Inland	118,440	1
	Private/Rental Ocean (≤3 mi)	3,654,698	23
	Private/Rental Ocean (>3 mi)	1,015,560	6
	Private/Rental Inland	4,262,060	26
	Total	16,230,274	
Louisiana	Shore Ocean (≤3 mi)	96,247	2
	Shore Inland	837,514	19
	Charter Ocean (≤3 mi)	11,845	0
	Charter Ocean (>3 mi)	56,052	1
	Charter Inland	108,181	2
	Private/Rental Ocean (≤3 mi)	166,798	4
	Private/Rental Ocean (>3 mi)	120,391	3
	Private/Rental Inland	3,094,252	69
	Total	4,491,280	
Mississippi	Shore Ocean (≤3 mi)	727	0
	Shore Inland	324,295	32
	Charter Ocean (≤3 mi)	3,928	0
	Charter Ocean (>3 mi)	68	0
	Charter Inland	3,058	0
	Private/Rental Ocean (≤3 mi)	25,895	3
	Private/Rental Ocean (>3 mi)	29,518	3
	Private/Rental Inland	610,422	61
	Total	997,911	
Gulf Total	Shore Ocean (≤3 mi)	4,475,518	19
	Shore Inland	4,730,144	20
	Charter Ocean (≤3 mi)	194,539	1
	Charter Ocean (>3 mi)	386,970	2
	Charter Inland	238,973	1
	Private/Rental Ocean (≤3 mi)	4,101,308	17
	Private/Rental Ocean (>3 mi)	1,350,460	6
	Private/Rental Inland	8,384,978	35
Total		23,862,890	

Source: USDOC, NMFS, 2007f.

In 2006, over 6.1 million people, up from 5.6 million in 2005, engaged in some form of recreational fishing in Louisiana, Mississippi, Alabama, and western Florida. Of the four states, western Florida had the highest number of anglers and fishing trips in 2005 and 2006, followed (in descending order by number of trips) by Louisiana, Alabama, and Mississippi. The most common mode of fishing in three Gulf Coast States was private/rental boats, comprising over 60 percent in Louisiana and Mississippi, and 26 percent in West Florida; the most popular form in Alabama was shore ocean (<3 mi) at 39 percent. In 2005 the most common mode of fishing in all Gulf Coast States was private/rental boats, comprising over 50 percent of the trips in each State.

In 2005 and 2006, the percentage of effort expended in inland, State, and Federal waters varied by State. In Mississippi and Louisiana, approximately 90 percent of trips were made in inland waters as opposed to State and Federal ocean waters in both 2005 and 2006. In West Florida and Alabama, the percentage of trips made in State ocean waters (46% and 51%, respectively) was much higher than the other two states. These percentages increased by 7 percent and 6 percent, respectively, from 2005.

The top species commonly caught by recreational fishers in the MRFSS Gulf Coast States are illustrated in **Table 5**. By number, herring and spotted sea trout, both inland species, were the most common fish caught by recreational anglers in the GOM during 2005 and 2006. In 2006, the estimated catch for herrings was over 41 million fish, up from 24 million in 2005; while anglers caught over 30 million spotted sea trout, up from 23 million in 2005. Other important inland species include red drum, saltwater catfishes, and pinfishes. In offshore oceanic waters of the GOM, the most important species in terms of pounds caught were red drum, red snapper, and sheepshead.

Hurricanes Katrina and Rita impacted recreational fishing from the Florida Panhandle to the Texas border, with additional impacts felt in southern Florida. The hurricanes had a major impact on the supporting infrastructure that anglers require to go fishing (e.g., bait shops, docks and marinas, lodging, fuel and ice facilities, etc.). In addition to damages to boats and facilities, revenue losses associated with lost markets of products or services are occurring. When considered on a regional basis, these lost market channels constitute a considerable reduction in the levels of economic activity, income generation, employment creation, and tax collections.

Storm-related recreational fisheries losses over the next year could total $421 million at the retail level (Louisiana Department of Wildlife and Fisheries, 2007). This figure includes losses incurred by licensed charter and guide vessels operating in the severely affected parishes.

In addition, Hurricanes Katrina and Rita deposited extensive amounts of debris over various areas of the Gulf Coast (USDOC, NOAA, 2007). Submerged marine debris poses a hazard to vessel traffic. The NOAA is conducting underwater surveys off the coasts of Louisiana, Mississippi, and Alabama. This information is being used by State and Federal agencies tasked with removing marine debris left by Hurricane Katrina, and it will aid in planning for the aftermath of future storms.

The MMS has reexamined the analysis for recreational fishing presented in the Multisale EIS, based on the additional information presented above. No new significant information was discovered that would alter the impact conclusion for recreational fishing presented in the Multisale EIS; therefore, a new analysis of the potential impacts of proposed Lease Sale 206 on recreational fishing is not required. The analysis and potential impacts detailed in the Multisale EIS still apply for proposed Lease Sale 206.

4.2.13. Recreational Resources

The description of the environment for recreational resources can be found in Chapter 3.3.3 of the Multisale EIS. Detailed analysis of the routine, accidental, and cumulative impacts of proposed Lease Sale 206 on recreational resources can be found in Chapters 4.2.2.1.13, 4.4.12, and 4.5.13, respectively. The following is a summary of the impact analysis from the Multisale EIS.

The northern GOM coastal zone is one of the major recreational regions of the U.S., particularly in connection with marine fishing and beach-related activities. The coastal beaches, barrier islands, estuarine bays and sounds, river deltas, and tidal marshes are used extensively and intensively for recreational activity by residents of the Gulf South and tourists from throughout the Nation, as well as from foreign countries. Commercial and private recreational facilities and establishments (such as resorts and marinas) also serve as primary interest areas and support services for people who seek enjoyment from the recreational resources associated with the GOM.

With respect to routine events, marine debris will be lost from time to time from operations resulting from proposed Lease Sale 206. The impact on Gulf Coast recreational beaches is expected to be minimal.

The incremental increase in helicopter and vessel traffic is expected to add very little additional noise that may affect beach users. Proposed Lease Sale 206 is expected to result in nearshore operations that may adversely affect the enjoyment of some Gulf Coast beach uses; however, these will have little effect on the number of beach users.

With respect to accidental events, it is unlikely that a spill would be a major threat to recreational beaches because any impacts would be short-term and localized. Should a spill contact a recreational beach, short-term displacement of recreational activity from the areas directly affected would occur. Beaches directly impacted would be expected to close for periods of 2-6 weeks or until the cleanup operations were complete. Should a spill result in a large volume of oil contacting a beach or a large recreational area being contacted by an oil slick, visitation to the area could be reduced by as much as 5-15 percent for as long as one season, but such an event should have no long-term effect on tourism. Tarballs can lessen the enjoyment of the recreational beaches but should have no long-term effect on the overall use of beaches.

With respect to cumulative events, debris and litter derived from both offshore and onshore sources are likely to diminish the tourist potential of beaches and to degrade the ambience of shoreline recreational activities, thereby affecting the enjoyment of recreational beaches throughout the area. The incremental beach trash resulting from proposed Lease Sale 206 is expected to be minimal. Platforms and drilling rigs operating nearshore may affect the ambience of recreational beaches, especially beach wilderness areas. The sound, sight, and wakes of OCS-related and non-OCS-related vessels, as well as OCS helicopters and other light aircraft traffic, are occasional distractions that are noticed by some beach users. Oil that contacts the coast may preclude short-term recreational use of one or more Gulf Coast beaches at the park or community levels. Displacement of recreational use from impacted areas will occur, and a short-term decline in tourism may result. Beach use at the regional level is unlikely to change from normal patterns; however, closure of specific beaches or parks directly impacted by a large oil spill is likely during cleanup operations. The incremental contribution of proposed Lease Sale 206 (as analyzed in Chapter 4.2.2.1.13 of the Multisale EIS) to the cumulative impact on recreational resources is minor due to the limited effect of increased helicopter, vessel traffic, and marine debris on the number of beach users.

A search was conducted for new information published since completion of the Multisale EIS. An Internet search of available literature was performed, including Federal and State agencies and industry websites. Research revealed the following new information.

Recreation and tourism are major sources of employment along the Gulf Coast. **Table 8** presents employment in tourism-related industries in 2005. The data in **Table 8** are a compilation of data from travel- and tourism-related industries in the County Business Patterns (USDOC, Bureau of the Census, 2007). Employment data are assumed to be in various travel-related industries, including: food and beverage stores, gas stations, general merchandise stores, passenger air transportation, transit and ground passenger transportation, scenic and sightseeing transportation, passenger car rental, travel arrangement and reservation services, arts/entertainment/recreation, and accommodation and food services. The data are only for coastal counties and parishes because they are the ones potentially affected by routine events, such as OCS-related air and vessel traffic, and accidental events, such as oil spills. This is different from the data for all counties and parishes in Labor Market Areas (LMA's) and Economic Impact Areas (EIA's) in Tables 3-15 and 3-16 in the Multisale EIS. The LMA's and EIA's extend inland geographically including inland counties and parishes not economically linked to the tourism and recreation of coastal counties. The data in **Table 8** more correctly describes the level of tourism-related employment and establishments potentially affected by OCS activities.

Beach visitation in Louisiana is low compared with other Gulf Coast States. Gambling is one of the most popular activities for nonresident visitors to Louisiana. In 2004, approximately 21 percent, down from 25 percent in 2002 and 23 percent in 2003, of nonresident visitors gambled on their trip to the State (Travel Industry Association of America, 2003-2005).

There are 16 casinos in Louisiana (14 riverboats, 1 land-based, and 1 racetrack), several of which are located along Louisiana's coast in Lake Charles, Houma, and the New Orleans area. The casinos generate nearly $2 billion in gaming revenues and approximately $414.2 million in tax revenues. The taxes are allocated among the general fund, the City of New Orleans, public retirement systems, State Capitol improvements, and a rainy day fund. It is estimated that Louisiana casinos admitted 37.5 million visitors and employed approximately 18,329 workers in 2003 (American Gaming Association, 2003).

Table 8

Employment and Establishments in Tourism Related Industries in 2005 by Coastal County and Parish

Area	Employment	Establishments	Area	Employment	Establishments
Texas			**Alabama**		
Cameron	20,192	1,046	Baldwin	13,084	690
Willacy	543	56	Mobile	26,101	1,322
Aransas	843	118	Alabama Total	39,185	2,012
Kenedy	10	1			
Kleberg	1,932	114	**Florida**		
Nueces	24,000	1,281	Bay	14,651	846
Refugio	414	22	Franklin	963	82
San Patricio	3,876	224	Gulf	561	51
Brazoria	12,962	686	Escambia	20,783	965
Matagorda	1,750	159	Okaloosa	17,768	824
Calhoun	1,148	94	Santa Rosa	6,569	321
Jackson	682	48	Walton	4,061	206
Jefferson	15,689	830	Jefferson	527	49
Chambers	1,205	896	Wakulla	849	68
Galveston	20,085	1,010	Taylor	1,118	80
Harris	253,614	11,700	Citrus	5,937	359
Texas Total	358,945	18,285	Dixie	378	46
			Levy	2,297	151
Louisiana			Hernando	8,283	388
Cameron	326	29	Hillsborough	92,467	3,678
Iberia	5,330	213	Pasco	19,798	1,016
Vermillion	1,996	158	Pinellas	68,259	3,568
Lafourche	5,391	299	Collier	30,501	1,191
St. Mary	4,622	201	Lee	43,592	1,860
Terrebonne	8,177	412	Miami-Dade	166,316	8,388
Orleans	56,900	1,972	Monroe	15,065	899
Plaquemines	1,317	110	Charlotte	9,126	414
St. Bernard	3,409	210	Manatee	17,546	907
St. Tammany	15,115	755	Sarasota	28,374	1,371
Louisiana Total	102,583	4,359	Florida Total	575,789	27,728
Mississippi			**Gulf States Total**	1,113,214	53,920
Hancock	3,623	160			
Harrison	26,209	764			
Jackson	6,880	612			
Mississippi Total	36,712	1,536			

Source: USDOC, Bureau of the Census, 2007.

For the year 2006, Mississippi had 27 operating casinos with a gross revenue of $2.57 billion and tax revenue of $302 million, with a visitor volume of over 35 million. Louisiana had 16 operating casinos with a gross revenue of $2.57 billion and tax revenue of $528 million, with a visitor volume of over 36 million (American Gaming Association, 2007).

Of the 12 casinos operating in the Biloxi-Gulfport Metropolitan Statistical Area, 10 were back in operation by December 2006 (Scott, 2007). For the Mississippi Gulf Coast (Gulfport and Biloxi), January 2007 gaming revenues were $106 million compared with $119 million for January 2005, and February 2007 revenues were $110 million compared with $109 million for February 2005 (Mississippi Gulf Coast Convention & Visitors Bureau, 2007).

During the 2005 hurricane season, Hurricanes Katrina and Rita inflicted severe damage on the Gulf Coast and deposited extensive amounts of debris over various areas of the Gulf Coast (USDOC, NOAA, 2007). Submerged marine debris poses a hazard to vessel traffic. The NOAA is conducting underwater surveys off the coasts of Louisiana, Mississippi, and Alabama. This information is being used by State and Federal agencies tasked with removing marine debris left by Hurricane Katrina and will aid in planning for the aftermath of future storms.

The Ocean Conservancy sponsors national and international beach cleanups, including annual events in Louisiana, Mississippi, and Alabama. The Louisiana event is coordinated by the Louisiana Department of Environmental Quality (LADEQ), Litter Reduction and Public Action Program. Statistics have not been published for the last Louisiana event, held on September 15, 2006 (LADEQ, 2007b). The Mississippi Marine Debris Task Force sponsors the annual Mississippi Coastal Cleanup. During the 18th Annual Mississippi Coastal Cleanup on September 16, 2006, volunteers collected over 63,111 pounds of trash along 147 mi (237 km) of Mississippi Gulf Coast and barrier islands. The 19th Annual Mississippi Coastal Cleanup is scheduled to take place on September 15, 2007 (Mississippi Alabama Sea Grant Consortium, 2007). The Alabama Coastal Cleanup is coordinated through the Alabama Department of Conservation and Natural Resources, State Lands Division, Coastal Section and the Alabama People Against a Littered State. Since joining the effort in 1987, 41,946 participants in Alabama have removed a total of 843,710 pounds of debris and cleaned 2,753 mi (4,431 km) of coastline (Alabama Coastal Cleanup, 2007).

The 1999-2000 National Survey on Recreation and the Environment (NSRE) is the first national survey to include a broad assessment of the Nation's participation in marine recreation (USDOC, NMFS, 2005). The 2005 NSRE surveys are currently underway.

The Multisale EIS presented data from the 2001 National Survey of Fishing, Hunting, and Wildlife-Associated Recreation for the five Gulf States (USDOI, FWS and USDOC, Bureau of the Census, 2001). The final 2006 survey findings will be released in November 2007 (USDOI, FWS, 2007d).

The MMS has reexamined the analysis for recreational resources presented in the Multisale EIS, based on the additional information presented above. No new significant information was discovered that would alter the impact conclusion for recreational resources presented in the Multisale EIS; therefore, a new analysis of the potential impacts of proposed Lease Sale 206 on recreational resources is not required. The analysis and potential impacts detailed in the Multisale EIS still apply for proposed Lease Sale 206.

4.2.14. Archaeological Resources

Archaeological resources are any material remains of human life or activities that are at least 50 years of age and that are of archaeological interest (30 CFR 250.105). The Archaeological Resources Regulation (30 CFR 250.194) provides specific authority to each MMS Regional Director to require archaeological resource surveys, analyses, and reports. Surveys are required prior to any exploration or development activities on leases within areas determined to have a high potential for archaeological resources (NTL's 2005-G07 and 2006-G07).

The description of archaeological resources (prehistoric and historic) can be found in Chapter 3.3.4 of the Multisale EIS. A detailed impact analysis of the routine, accidental, and cumulative impacts of proposed Lease Sale 206 on archaeological resources can be found in Chapters 4.2.2.1.14, 4.4.13, and 4.5.14 of the Multisale EIS, respectively. The following information is a summary of the impact analysis incorporated from the Multisale EIS.

The greatest potential impact to archaeological resources as a result of proposed Lease Sale 206 would result from direct contact between an offshore activity (platform installation, drilling rig emplacement, and dredging or pipeline project) and a prehistoric site located on the continental shelf or an historic shipwreck. The NTL for archaeological resource surveys in the GOM Region, NTL 2005-G07, mandates a 300-m linespacing for areas having the potential for containing prehistoric sites on the continental shelf, 50-m linespacing for remote-sensing surveys of leases within the areas having high potential for historic shipwrecks in water depths 200 m (656 ft) or less, and 300-m linespacing of leases within the areas having high potential for historic shipwrecks in water depths greater than 200 m (656 ft). NTL 2006-G07 identifies those lease blocks that have been designated as having a high potential for containing archaeological resources.

The archaeological survey and archaeological clearance of sites required prior to an operator beginning oil and gas activities on a lease are expected to be highly effective at identifying possible archaeological resources. Since the survey and clearance provide a significant reduction in the potential for a damaging interaction between an impact-producing factor and an archaeological resource, there is a very small possibility of an OCS activity contacting an archaeological resource. Should such contact occur, there would be damage to or loss of significant and/or unique archaeological information.

Spills, collisions, and blowouts are accidental events that can happen in association with a proposed activity in the Lease Sale 206 area. If an accidental event occurs as a result of one of these events, there could be an impact to archaeological resources. Oil spills have the potential to affect both prehistoric and historic archaeological resources. Impacts to historic resources would be limited to visual impacts and, possibly, physical impacts associated with spill cleanup operations. Impacts to prehistoric archaeological sites would be the result of hydrocarbon contamination of organic materials, which have the potential to date site occupation through radiocarbon dating techniques, as well as possible physical disturbance associated with spill cleanup operations. Since archaeological sites are protected under law, it is expected that any spill cleanup operations would be conducted in such a way as to cause little or no impacts to archaeological resources. Visual impacts to coastal historic sites would be temporary and reversible; however, should an oil spill directly contact a coastal prehistoric site, unique or significant archaeological information could be lost, and this impact would be irreversible.

The cumulative analysis considers the effects of impact-producing factors related to proposed Lease Sale 206, OCS activities in the cumulative activity area, trawling, sport diving, commercial treasure hunting, seismic exploration in State waters, and tropical storms on archaeological resources. Specific types of impact-producing factors associated with OCS activities that are considered in this analysis include drilling rig and platform emplacement, pipeline emplacement, anchoring, oil spills, dredging, new onshore facilities, and ferromagnetic debris. Archaeological surveys are assumed to be highly effective in reducing the potential for an interaction between an impact-producing activity and archaeological resources.

Onshore development associated with activities from this lease proposed sale could result in the direct physical contact between the construction of new onshore facilities or pipeline canals and previously unidentified historic or prehistoric sites. This direct physical contact with a historic site could cause physical damage to, or complete destruction of, information on the history of the region and the Nation. Direct physical contact with a prehistoric site could destroy fragile artifacts or site features and could disturb the site context. The result would be the loss of information on the prehistory of North America and the Gulf Coast region. Facilities that are projected to be constructed as a result of this lease proposed sale must receive approval from the pertinent Federal, State, county/parish, and/or communities. Protection of archaeological resources in these cases is expected to be achieved through the various approval processes involved. There is, therefore, no expected impact to onshore historic or prehistoric sites adjacent to the Lease Sale 206 area from onshore development.

Recent hurricane activity in the GOM is certain to have impacted archaeological resources in shallow water. A search was conducted for new information published since completion of the Multisale EIS; however, little new information was identified. Yet, it is almost certain that any shipwrecks within the path of Hurricanes Katrina or Rita in shallow water were impacted to some extent by these storms. In September 2005 the National Park Service (NPS) conducted a study of sites along the Gulf Coast that were impacted by Hurricane Katrina (USDOI, NPS, 2005). This assessment identified three types of damage that can occur to archaeological sites: tree throws; storm surge, scouring and erosion; and seabed shifting. On the OCS, the two primary types of damage would be associated with storm surge and seabed shifting. Damage from either of these activities could adversely affect both prehistoric and historic sites on the OCS.

A recently published report, *Archaeological and Biological Analysis of World War II Shipwrecks in the Gulf of Mexico: Artificial Reef Effect in Deep Water* (Church et al., 2007), documents the results of a multidisciplinary study that focused on the biological and archaeological aspects of seven World War II era shipwrecks in the north-central portion of the Gulf of Mexico. The study was funded by MMS and NOAA's Office of Ocean Exploration.

Seven shipwrecks, including a German U-2 submarine and some of its targets, were investigated. The ships lie in water ranging from 122 to 1,981 m (400 to 6,500 ft) deep. The study found deep-sea wrecks act as artificial reefs, attracting far more species of plants and animals than expected. The finding indicates that oil and gas production platforms in deep water are likely to serve as hard surface, supporting hundreds of life forms.

Wrecks in moderate depths gave researchers clear evidence of many rare and uncommon invertebrate species in close proximity to the wrecks and on the wrecks themselves. The number of species and individuals declined rapidly in proportion to distance away from the wrecks, showing that these wrecks form an attractive habitat for many kinds of marine life. Wrecks at these intermediate depths had 50 percent more species than those in shallower water or deeper water. Shallower water wrecks, likely because of turbidity, and deeper water wrecks because of the extreme conditions of cold, darkness, and pressure, hosted a smaller number of species.

The scientists reported, among other findings, that the diversity of fish species generally decreases with depth. At the shallower water wrecks, where corals were growing, reef fishes were present. At the deepest water wrecks, no corals were found nor were community structure and fish density significantly different over the wrecks as opposed to away from them. Therefore, scientists conclude that, in the deepest water, the upper levels of offshore platforms will attract considerable marine life, but the platforms are not likely to attract fish at their deepest levels. The marine archaeology part of the study positively confirmed the identity of three wrecks and found a relationship among water depth, ship size, and the size of the debris field. The state of preservation of the wrecks was correlated with water depth. No wreck was found to be contaminating or adversely affecting the area around them.

The MMS recently awarded a study to investigate the impacts that recent storm activity may have had on historic shipwrecks in the Gulf of Mexico. Remote-sensing surveys for this study were completed in May 2007 and dive operations will be carried out in October 2007, with a final report of findings expected early in 2009. Preliminary analysis of the remote-sensing surveys indicates that at least 3 of the 10 shipwrecks examined were affected by recent storm activity. Further analysis will occur after diving operations are complete in October 2007 (PBS&J, in preparation).

The MMS has reexamined the analysis for archaeological resources presented in the Multisale EIS, based on the additional information presented above. No new significant information was discovered that would alter the impact conclusion for archaeological resources presented in the Multisale EIS; therefore, a new analysis of the potential impacts of proposed Lease Sale 206 on archaeological resources is not required. The analysis and potential impacts detailed in the Multisale EIS still apply for proposed Lease Sale 206.

4.2.15. Human Resources and Land Use

4.2.15.1. Land Use and Coastal Infrastructure

Land use and OCS-related coastal infrastructure in the analysis area are discussed in Chapters 3.3.5.1.2 and 3.3.5.8 of the Multisale EIS and include the following: service bases, navigation channels, helicopter hubs, construction facilities, processing facilities, terminals, waste disposal and storage facilities, coastal pipelines, and coastal barging. A detailed impact analysis of the routine, accidental, and cumulative impacts of proposed Lease Sale 206 on land use and coastal infrastructure can be found in Chapters 4.2.2.1.15.1, 4.4.14.1, and 4.5.15.1 of the Multisale EIS, respectively. The following is a summary of the impact analysis incorporated from the Multisale EIS.

Proposed Lease Sale 206 would not require additional coastal infrastructure, with the exception of possibly one new gas processing facility and one new pipeline landfall, and would not alter the current land use of the analysis area. There may be some expansion at current facilities, but the land in the analysis area is sufficient to handle such development. There is also sufficient land to construct a new gas processing plant in the analysis area, if necessary in the future. Accidental events such as oil or chemical spills, blowouts, and vessel collisions would have no effects on land use. Coastal or nearshore spills could have short-term adverse effects on coastal infrastructure requiring clean up of any oil or chemicals spilled.

Activities relating to the OCS Program and State production are expected to minimally affect the analysis area's land use. Land use in the analysis area will evolve over time; most changes are likely to occur as a result of general regional growth rather than activities associated with the OCS Program and State production. Projected new coastal infrastructure by state as a result of the OCS Program is shown in Table 4-9 of the Multisale EIS. While it is possible that up to 14 new, greenfield gas processing facilities could be developed, it is much more likely that a large share of the natural gas processing capacity that will be needed in the industry will be located at existing facilities, using future investments for expansions and/or to replace depreciated capital equipment. It is likely that few (if any) new plants would be developed along the Central or Western GOM. Any changes to supporting infrastructure (mostly facility expansions, except for the 4-6 new pipeline shore facilities and any new, greenfield gas processing plants) are expected to be contained on available land. Most subareas in the analysis area have strong industrial bases and designated industrial parks to accommodate future growth in oil and gas businesses.

Port Fourchon is expected to experience significant impacts to its land use from OCS-related expansion. Increased OCS-related usage from port clients is expected to significantly impact LA Hwy 1 in Lafourche Parish. Also, increased demand of water by the OCS will further strain Lafourche Parish's water system. It is assumed that the Louisiana Department of Natural Resources' existing procedures to identify potential regulatory and restoration conflicts will continue to be utilized, including current requirements that any project proposed within ¼ mi from either an active or proposed restoration project be reviewed to determine if it would interfere or have adverse effects on the restoration project (USACOE, 2004). Therefore, new coastal infrastructure that may result from proposed Lease Sale 206 or the OCS Program would not interfere with active or proposed restoration projects.

As stated in Chapter 4.1.2.1.7 of the Multisale EIS, MMS assumes that most new OCS pipelines will connect to existing pipelines in Federal and State waters, and result in few, if any, new pipeline landfalls. Up to one new pipeline landfall was projected as the result of proposed Lease Sale 206, and 32-47 new pipeline landfalls were projected as a result of the OCS Program from 2007 to 2046.

The MMS recently analyzed historical data to validate past scenario projections, including projects of new pipeline landfalls (USDOI, MMS, 2007e). This analysis confirms MMS's assumption that the majority of new pipelines constructed would connect to the existing infrastructure in Federal and State waters and that very few would result in new pipeline landfalls. Most pipeline landfalls in the GOM transport production resulting from more than one lease sale; therefore, an OCS pipeline landfall could rarely be attributed to a single lease sale. Multiple factors have influenced the decrease in the number of new pipeline landfalls. Therefore, MMS's projection of up to one new pipeline landfall per lease sale may be too high. Although there will be some instances where new pipelines may need to be constructed, there is nothing to suggest any dramatic shifts in the trends in new landfalls given the current outlook for GOM development, particularly in coastal Louisiana.

The term "pipeline shore facility" is a broad term describing the onshore location where the first stage of processing occurs for OCS pipelines carrying different combinations of oil, condensate, gas, and produced water. A pipeline shore facility may support one or several pipelines. In Chapter 4.1.2.1.5.1 of the Multisale EIS, no new pipeline shore facilities are projected as a result of proposed Lease Sale 206. As a result of the OCS Program, new shore facilities may be needed to support new larger oil pipeline landfalls. A total of 4-6 new pipeline shore facilities are projected as a result of the OCS Program.

The MMS has reexamined the analysis for land use and coastal infrastructure presented in the Multisale EIS, based on the additional information presented above. No new significant information was discovered that would alter the impact conclusion for land use and coastal infrastructure presented in the Multisale EIS; therefore, a new analysis of the potential impacts of proposed Lease Sale 206 on land use and coastal infrastructure is not required. The analysis and potential impacts detailed in the Multisale EIS still apply for proposed Lease Sale 206.

4.2.15.2. Demographics

The description of the environment for demographics is described in Chapter 3.3.5.4 of the Multisale EIS. Detailed analysis of the routine, accidental, and cumulative impacts of proposed Lease Sale 206 on demographics is presented in Chapters 4.2.2.1.15.2, 4.4.14.2, and 4.5.15.2 of the Multisale EIS, respectively. The following is a summary of the impact analysis from the Multisale EIS.

Routine activities relating to proposed Lease Sale 206 are expected to affect minimally the analysis area's land use, infrastructure, and demography. These impacts are projected to mirror employment effects that are estimated to be negligible to any one EIA (**Figure 5**). Baseline patterns and distributions of these factors, as described in Chapter 3.3.5.4 of the Multisale EIS, are expected to approximately maintain the same level. Changes in land use throughout the analysis area are expected to be contained and minimal. The OCS-related infrastructure is in place and will not change as a result of proposed Lease Sale 206. Current baseline estimates of population growth for the analysis area show a continuation of growth, but at a slower rate.

Figure 5.   Economic Impact Areas in the Gulf of Mexico.

Accidental events associated with proposed Lease Sale 206 such as oil or chemical spills, blowouts, and vessel collisions would have no effects on the demographic characteristics of the Gulf coastal communities.

The cumulative effects of human and natural activities in the coastal area have severely degraded the deltaic processes and shifted the coastal area from a condition of net land building to one of net landloss. As inland marshes and barrier islands erode or subside, without effective restoration efforts, the population in coastal communities in southern Louisiana is expected to shift to the more northern portions of the parishes and cause increasing populations in urban and suburban areas and declining populations in rural coastal areas (USACOE, 2004).

Cumulative activities related to the OCS Program are expected to affect minimally the analysis area's demography. Baseline patterns and distributions of these factors, as described in Chapter 3.3.5.4.1 of the Multisale EIS, are not expected to change for the analysis area as a whole. The baseline population patterns are expected to change for the eight counties and parishes that were most negatively affected by the 2005 hurricane season (see Chapter 3.3.5.4 of the Multisale EIS for a discussion of these changes). Some regions within Louisiana EIA's, Port Fourchon in particular, are expected to experience some impacts to population and their education system as a result of increased demand for OCS labor. As discussed in Chapter 4.2.2.1.15.2 of the Multisale EIS, proposed Lease Sale 206 is expected have an incremental contribution of less than 1 percent to the population level in any of the EIA's. Given both the low levels of population growth and industrial expansion associated with proposed Lease Sale 206, the baseline age and racial distribution pattern and education status, is expected to continue through the year 2046.

In the Multisale EIS, MMS used data from Woods & Poole's *Complete Economic and Demographic Data Source* (Woods & Poole Economics, Inc., 2006) for baseline population and employment estimates over the 40-year life of a typical proposed CPA lease sale. The 2007 Woods & Poole data became available in late August 2007 and contains their revised estimates regarding the economic and demographic impacts of the 2005 hurricanes on the Gulf region (Woods & Poole Economics, Inc., 2007). In the new data, population, income, and employment were assumed to decline from 2005 to 2006 by 76 percent in St. Bernard Parish, Louisiana; 51 percent in Orleans Parish, Louisiana; 22 percent in Plaquemines Parish, Louisiana; 19 percent in Cameron Parish; Louisiana; 13 percent in Hancock County, Mississippi; and 11 percent in Harrison County, Mississippi. In each case, these losses were less than those that were assumed in the Woods & Poole 2006 data. The 2007 data also have revised assumptions regarding counties and parishes that experienced population and employment gains because of Hurricane

Katrina displacement: 9 percent in Pearl River County, Mississippi; 7 percent in Tangipahoa Parish, Louisiana; 5 percent in St. John the Baptist Parish, Louisiana; 5 percent in East Baton Rouge Parish, Louisiana; and 4 percent in St. Charles Parish, Louisiana from 2005 to 2006. In each case, these gains were less than those that were assumed in the 2006 data.

As discussed in **Chapter 4.1.1**, the exploration and development activity scenarios used in the Multisale EIS for a typical CPA sale remain unchanged and are used for the analysis of proposed Lease Sale 206. Consequently, the population projections for a typical proposed CPA sale in Table 4-28 of the Multisale EIS are unchanged for proposed Lease Sale 206. The MMS reanalyzed the high-case population impacts on a percentage basis for the three EIA's that exhibited the highest impacts in the Multisale EIS (LA-2, LA-3, and LA-4) using the revised Woods & Poole data. With the exception of year 1 (2008) for LA-4, which declined slightly, the population impacts on a percentage basis for the three EIA's are the same as reported in Table 4-29 of the Multisale EIS. Thus, the potential population impacts described in the Multisale EIS and summarized above apply for proposed Lease Sale 206.

A search was conducted for new information published since completion of the Multisale EIS. Research of all references for demographics in the Multisale EIS revealed the following new information.

The following information is summarized from Rowley (2007).

The Louisiana Public Health Institute (LPHI) estimated the City of New Orleans's population at 191,139 in January 2007, the U.S. Census Bureau estimated the population at 223,388 in July 2006, and the City estimates it closer to 230,000. For St. Bernard Parish, the Census Bureau estimated the population at 66,441 in 2000 and 15,514 in July 2006, and the LPHI estimates it at 25,296 in January 2007.

Hurricane Katrina flooded more than 40 percent of Hancock County, Mississippi, which suffered the most of any of the Gulf Coast communities. Prior to Hurricane Katrina the Hancock County population was 46,546; as of July 2006, the Census estimated it at 40,421, indicating a substantial return of population. The Jefferson Parish population estimates are 451,049 in 2000, 431,361 in July 2006, and 434,666 in January 2007. The high population in Jefferson Parish indicates an in-migration of former residents of Orleans, St. Bernard, and Plaquemines Parishes and seasonal construction workers. See Chapter 3.3.5.5.1 of the Multisale EIS for the relationship of population to housing availability and employment.

A year and a half after Hurricanes Katrina and Rita, the recovery was uneven throughout the areas originally affected (Rowley, 2007). Areas where the most severe problems remain are New Orleans and St. Bernard Parish, Louisiana; and Hancock County, Mississippi. Recovery is well underway in Jefferson Parish, Lake Charles, and Cameron Parish, Louisiana; and Biloxi, Gulfport, and Pascagoula, Mississippi; and Bayou La Batre, Alabama. Recovery is driving expansion in East Baton Rouge and St. Tammany Parishes, Louisiana; Jackson, Hattiesburg, and Laurel Mississippi; and Gulf Shores and Mobile, Alabama. The measures of recovery are the functions of local government, population, crime, economic and fiscal effects, local government budgets, housing, and labor.

The MMS has reexamined the analysis for demographics presented in the Multisale EIS, based on the additional information presented above. No new significant information was discovered that would alter the impact conclusion for demographics presented in the Multisale EIS; therefore, a new analysis of the potential impacts of proposed Lease Sale 206 on demographics is not required. The analysis and potential impacts detailed in the Multisale EIS still apply for proposed Lease Sale 206.

4.2.15.3. *Economic Factors*

The description of the current economic factors for the GOM analysis area can be found in Chapter 3.3.5.5 of the Multisale EIS. A detailed impact analysis of the routine, accidental, and cumulative impacts of proposed Lease Sale 206 on economic factors can be found in Chapters 4.2.2.1.15.3, 4.4.14.3, and 4.5.15.3 of the Multisale EIS, respectively. The following is a summary of the impact analysis incorporated from the Multisale EIS.

Should proposed Lease Sale 206 occur, there would be only minor economic changes in the Texas, Louisiana, Mississippi, Alabama, and Florida EIA's (**Figure 5**). Proposed Lease Sale 206 is expected to generate less than a 1 percent increase in employment in any of these subareas. This demand will be met primarily with the existing population and available labor force. Accidental events such as oil or chemical spills, blowouts, and vessel collisions could have modest, short-term adverse economic consequences. Negative, long-term economic and social impacts may be more substantial if fishing, shrimping, oystering, and/or tourism were to suffer or were to be perceived as having suffered because of the event.

The OCS Program will produce only minor economic changes in most of the individual EIA's. However, it is projected to substantially impact the Louisiana EIA's LA-2 and LA-3, with OCS-related employment expected to peak at 23.8 percent and 9.8 percent of total employment, respectively. On a regional level, activities related to the OCS Program are expected to significantly impact employment in Lafourche Parish, Louisiana, within EIA LA-3. Therefore, the population, housing, roads (LA Hwy 1), water supply, schools, and hospitals in the parish will be affected and potentially strained.

A search was conducted for new information published since completion of the Multisale EIS. A search of Internet information sources as well as personal communication with regional and national economic experts was conducted to determine the availability of new information that would affect the impact analyses.

In the Multisale EIS, MMS used data from Woods & Poole's *Complete Economic and Demographic Data Source* (Woods & Poole Economics, Inc., 2006) for baseline population and employment estimates over the 40-year life of a typical proposed CPA lease sale. The 2007 Woods & Poole data became available in late August 2007 and contains their revised estimates regarding the economic and demographic impacts of the 2005 hurricanes on the Gulf region (Woods & Poole Economics, Inc., 2007). In the new data, population, income, and employment were assumed to decline from 2005 to 2006 by 76 percent in St. Bernard Parish, Louisiana; 51 percent in Orleans Parish, Louisiana; 22 percent in Plaquemines Parish, Louisiana; 19 percent in Cameron Parish; Louisiana; 13 percent in Hancock County, Mississippi; and 11 percent in Harrison County, Mississippi. In each case, these losses were less than those that were assumed in the Woods & Poole 2006 data. The 2007 data also have revised assumptions regarding counties and parishes that experienced population and employment gains because of Hurricane Katrina displacement: 9 percent in Pearl River County, Mississippi; 7 percent in Tangipahoa Parish, Louisiana; 5 percent in St. John the Baptist Parish, Louisiana; 5 percent in East Baton Rouge Parish, Louisiana; and 4 percent in St. Charles Parish, Louisiana from 2005 to 2006. In each case, these gains were less than those that were assumed in the 2006 data.

As discussed in **Chapter 4.1.1**, the exploration and development activity scenarios used in the Multisale EIS for a typical CPA sale remain unchanged and are used for the analysis of proposed Lease Sale 206. Consequently, the employment projections for a typical proposed CPA sale in the Multisale EIS (Tables 4-30 and 4-31) are unchanged for Lease Sale 206. The MMS reanalyzed the high-case employment impacts on a percentage basis for the three economic impact areas (EIA's) that exhibited the highest impacts in the Multisale EIS (LA-2, LA-3, and LA-4) using the revised Woods & Poole data. As shown in **Table 9** below, with the exception of year 1 (2008) for LA-4, which declined slightly, the employment impacts on a percentage basis for the three EIA's are the same as reported in Table 4-32 of the Multisale EIS. Thus, the potential employment impacts described in the Multisale EIS and summarized above apply for proposed Lease Sale 206.

Table 9

Projected Employment Associated with Proposed Lease Sale 206 by Economic Impact Area

Calendar Year	Model Year	Revised Baseline Employment Projections[1]			High Case CPA Proposed Action Employment Estimates[2]			Projected Employment Associated with Proposed Lease Sale 206 as Percent of Total Baseline Employment		
		LA2	LA3	LA4	LA2	LA3	LA4	LA2	LA3	LA4
2005		301,335	612,652	763,607						
2006		308,367	635,014	594,135						
2007		312,413	643,811	612,015						
2008	1	316,465	652,584	629,890	572	550	355	0.18%	0.08%	0.06%
2009	2	320,517	661,360	647,766	1,507	1,477	998	0.47%	0.22%	0.15%
2010	3	324,566	670,138	665,642	1,442	1,353	902	0.44%	0.20%	0.14%
2011	4	328,615	678,909	683,518	1,486	1,394	938	0.45%	0.21%	0.14%
2012	5	332,671	687,676	701,383	3,602	3,482	2,354	1.08%	0.51%	0.34%
2013	6	336,719	696,450	719,259	1,719	1,589	1,065	0.51%	0.23%	0.15%
2014	7	340,770	705,217	737,139	1,232	1,140	779	0.36%	0.16%	0.11%
2015	8	344,814	713,975	755,004	1,080	921	617	0.31%	0.13%	0.08%
2020	13	365,080	757,783	844,358	1,083	830	580	0.30%	0.11%	0.07%
2025	18	385,340	801,553	933,709	1,197	898	639	0.31%	0.11%	0.07%
2030	23	405,612	845,271	1,023,030	1,088	798	571	0.27%	0.09%	0.06%

[1] Source: Woods & Poole Economics, Inc., 2007.
[2] Source: Tables 4-31a and 4-31b of the Multisale EIS.

Additional supplemental information is available regarding current economic conditions in the GOM region, particularly as it relates the recovery to date from the 2005 hurricanes. However, this new information (summarized below) does not in any way change the baseline population and employment projections used to analyze impacts of a typical CPA sale and the OCS Program, the methodologies used, or the conclusions presented in the Multisale EIS.

Two years after Hurricanes Katrina and Rita the recovery remains uneven throughout the areas originally affected. Areas where the most severe problems remain are Orleans and St. Bernard Parishes, Louisiana, and Hancock County, Mississippi. Affordable housing continues to be a problem in these areas, particularly in New Orleans. Adding to the problem is the high cost of insurance and building materials, causing many prospective developers to postpone projects until these issues are better resolved. Recovery is well underway in Jefferson and Calcasieu Parishes, Louisiana, as well as in Biloxi, Gulfport, and Pascagoula, Mississippi; and Bayou La Batre, Alabama. Recovery is driving expansion in East Baton Rouge and St. Tammany Parishes in Louisiana; Jackson, Hattiesburg, and Laurel, Mississippi; and in Gulf Shores and Mobile, Alabama. The measures of recovery are the functions of local government, population, crime, economic and fiscal effects, local government budgets, housing, and labor (Rowley, 2007).

Researchers continue to study the employment impacts of the 2005 hurricane season. The Bureau of Labor Statistics did a special review of the employment impacts of Hurricane Katrina and found that St. Bernard, Orleans, and Jefferson Parishes had the largest percent declines in employment between September 2004 and September 2006 (38%, 27%, and 24.5%, respectively). In the two months following Hurricane Katrina, nonfarm payroll employment in Louisiana fell by 241,000, a decline of 12 percent; in the New Orleans metro area, employment declined by 215,000, or 35 percent. In the New Orleans metro area in June 2006, it was 30 percent below the level a year earlier. Total nonfarm employment in Louisiana decreased by 184,600 jobs or 9.6 percent from September 2004 to September 2005, and in May 2006, the year-to-year loss was 177,700 jobs or 9.1 percent (U.S. Dept. of Labor, Bureau of Labor Statistics, 2006; pages 2, 4, 6, 8, 27, and 28). However, more recent data show nonfarm payroll employment in Louisiana increasing 3.8 percent between April 2006 and April 2007 (one of the largest over-the-year percentage gains in employment for a State), or an increase of 69,500 from 1,835,700 to 1,905,200 (U.S. Dept. of Labor, Bureau of Labor Statistics, 2007).

Estimating employment data has proven more difficult post-Katrina, and some previous estimates are being revised as data-gathering limitations are addressed. For example, the Atlanta Federal Reserve Bank announced a revision to their employment estimates for Louisiana from 1,766,400 to 1,844,300 (an increase of 77,900 or 4.4%) between March 2005 and March 2006. Much of the revision was to account for job growth in the State's construction industry that had been underestimated due to survey sampling issues (such as identifying and sampling new construction businesses). Professional and business services is another industry where employment in Louisiana appears to have been originally underestimated (Federal Reserve Bank of Atlanta, 2006).

Researchers also continue to examine the impacts of the 2005 hurricane season on businesses in the region. For example, a Louisiana State University report on the hurricanes' effect on businesses comparing the second quarter of 2005 with the second quarter of 2006 concludes that, after a decline of over 5,000 in the number of employers (5.3%), the entire State of Louisiana had 2,270 fewer employers (2.3%) one year after the hurricanes (Terrell and Bilbo, 2007). The business failure rate in the year after the storms was 11.7 percent for the State as a whole compared with 26.5 percent for the five parish Southeast region.

The MMS has reexamined the analysis for economic factors presented in the Multisale EIS, based on the additional information presented above. No new significant information was discovered that would alter the impact conclusion for economic factors presented in the Multisale EIS; therefore, a new analysis of the potential impacts of proposed Lease Sale 206 on economic factors is not required. The analysis and potential impacts detailed in the Multisale EIS still apply for proposed Lease Sale 206.

4.2.15.4. Environmental Justice

The description of the environment for environmental justice can be found in Chapter 3.3.5.10 of the Multisale EIS. Detailed analysis of the routine, accidental, and cumulative impacts of proposed Lease Sale 206 on environmental justice can be found in Chapters 4.2.2.1.15.4, 4.4.14.4, and 4.5.15.4, respectively. The following is a summary of the impact analysis from the Multisale EIS.

Because of the presence of an extensive and widespread support system for OCS and associated labor force, the effects of proposed Lease Sale 206 are expected to be widely distributed and, except in Louisiana, little felt. In general, the infrastructural needs generated by proposed Lease Sale 206 will be met by the existing support systems, and these effects will be negligible. In general, who will be hired and where new infrastructure might be located is impossible to predict. A new C-Port (multiservices port terminal facility) in Galveston may be developed and this would likely increase Texas' share of the effects. However, this would occur in an already highly industrialized area so its effects would be primarily economic. For these reasons, impacts related to proposed Lease Sale 206 are expected to be economic and have a limited but positive effect on low-income and minority populations. Given the existing distribution of the industry and the limited concentrations of minority and low-income peoples, proposed Lease Sale 206 is not expected to have a disproportionate effect on these populations.

Lafourche Parish, Louisiana, will experience the most concentrated effects of proposed Lease Sale 206; however, because the parish is not heavily low-income or minority and because the effects of road traffic and port expansion will not occur in areas of low-income or minority concentration, these groups are not expected to be affected differentially.

Proposed Lease Sale 206 would help to maintain ongoing levels of activity rather than expand them. Future changes in activity levels will most likely be caused by fluctuations in oil prices and imports, and not be activities related to proposed Lease Sale 206. Routine impacts associated with proposed Lease Sale 206 are not expected to have disproportionate high/adverse environmental or health effects on minority or low-income populations.

With respect to accidental events, considering the low likelihood of an oil spill and the heterogeneous population distribution along the GOM region, accidental spill events associated with proposed Lease Sale 206 are not expected to have disproportionate adverse environmental or health effects on minority or low-income people.

In the GOM coastal area, the contribution of proposed Lease Sale 206 and the OCS Program to the cumulative effects of all activities and trends affecting environmental justice issues over the next 40 years is expected to be negligible to minor. The cumulative effects will be concentrated in coastal areas, and particularly, Louisiana. Most OCS Program effects are expected to be in the areas of job creation and the stimulation of the economy and are expected to make a small yet positive contribution to an area's economy. The contribution of the cumulative OCS Program to the cumulative impacts of all factors affecting environmental justice is expected to be minor (USDOI, MMS, 2001); therefore, the incremental contribution of proposed Lease Sale 206 to the cumulative impacts would also be minor.

A search was conducted for new information published since completion of the Multisale EIS. Analysis of FEMA storm damage data shows that Hurricane Katrina's impact was disproportionately borne by the region's African American community, by people who rented their homes, and by the poor and unemployed. More than one-third of the region's 1.7 million residents lived in areas that suffered flooding or moderate to catastrophic storm damage, according to FEMA. The majority of people living in damaged areas were in the City of New Orleans (over 350,000), with additional concentrations in suburban Jefferson Parish (175,000) and St. Bernard Parish (53,000) and along the Mississippi Coast (54,000). In the region as a whole, the disparities in storm damage are shown in the following comparisons (arranged in order of the degree of disparity): by race–damaged areas were 46 percent black, compared with 26 percent in undamaged areas; by housing tenure–46 percent of homes in damaged areas were occupied by renters, compared with 31 percent in undamaged communities; and by poverty and employment status–21 percent of households had incomes below the poverty line in damaged areas, compared with 15 percent in undamaged areas, and 7.6 percent of persons in the labor force were unemployed in damaged areas (before the storm), compared to 6.0 percent in undamaged areas. These comparisons are heavily influenced by the experience of the City of New Orleans. Outside the city, there were actually smaller shares of African American, poor, and unemployed residents in the damaged areas. Closer inspection of neighborhoods within New Orleans shows that some affluent white neighborhoods were hard hit, while some poor minority neighborhoods were spared. Yet, if the post-Katrina city were limited to the population previously living in areas that were undamaged by the storm – that is, if nobody were able to return to damaged neighborhoods – New Orleans is at risk of losing more than 80 percent of its black population (Logan, 2007).

The Multisale EIS states the following: "Evidence also suggests that a healthy offshore petroleum industry also indirectly benefits low-income and minority populations." One MMS study in Louisiana found income inequality decreased during the oil boom and increased with the decline (Tolbert, 1995). The following updated information relates to this point.

A follow-up study to Tolbert (1995) about Abbeville, Louisiana, resulted in the following findings. A study component of a plant closure in Abbeville found that more employment opportunities exist within the community and surrounding area because, indirectly, growth of the oil and gas industry has served as an impetus in creating other labor market opportunities. A study component of industrial composition finds that a key source of sustainability from economic fluctuations at one time may be problematic at another time. Conversely, a problematic sector of the local economy at one time period may be proven to be a stabilizing sector at another time. These sectors include the oil and gas industry, manufacturing, and others. The particular lesson in the Abbeville context is that shifting sectors can be sustained by strong business services and professional sectors. Industrial diversity in Abbeville is dynamic overtime. The conclusions of Tolbert (2006) appear to qualify the conclusions of Tolbert (1995).

The MMS has reexamined the analysis for environmental justice presented in the Multisale EIS, based on the additional information presented above. No new significant information was discovered that would alter the impact conclusion for environmental justice presented in the Multisale EIS; therefore, a new analysis of the potential impacts of proposed Lease Sale 206 on environmental justice is not required. The analysis and potential impacts detailed in the Multisale EIS still apply for proposed Lease Sale 206.

5. CONSULTATION AND COORDINATION

5.1. SCOPING FOR THE ENVIRONMENTAL ASSESSMENT FOR THE CENTRAL PLANNING AREA'S PROPOSED LEASE SALE 206

The MMS performs ongoing external and internal scoping in order to determine the breadth and depth necessary for environmental analysis.

External Scoping: The scoping process for this EA was formally initiated on June 22, 2007, with the *Federal Register* notice announcing the preparation of an EA. In the notice, MMS requested that interested parties submit comments regarding any new information or issues that should be addressed in the EA. The comment period closed on July 23, 2007. One response was received from the Governor of Alabama. This comment was considered in the preparation of this EA.

Scoping and coordination efforts continue throughout the lease sale process and have been conducted since the publication of the Multisale EIS:

- On March 1 and 8, 2007, scoping meetings were held to solicit comments regarding new information or issues that should be addressed in the Draft Supplemental EIS (SEIS) for EPA Lease Sale 224 in Pensacola, Florida, and Larose, Louisiana.

- On April 10, 2007, MMS sent the Consistency Determinations (CD) for WPA Lease Sale 204 to the States of Texas and Louisiana, documenting the consistency of the proposed sale with the coastal zone management (CZM) programs of those states. The States' comments on Lease Sale 204 were due in writing on June 10, 2007. The State of Texas did not respond within the 60-day comment period; therefore, MMS presumed the State's concurrence with the CD pursuant to the provisions of regulations at 15 CFR 930.41(a). In a letter dated June 7, 2007, the State of Louisiana requested a 15-day extension pursuant to 15 CFR 930.41(b). The MMS approved the requested extension on June 11, 2007; this extended the date for the end of the State's comment period to June 25, 2007. In a letter dated June 25, 2007, the State of Louisiana provided comments on the CD for Lease Sale 204. The State asked for a cooperative agreement with MMS to establish procedures for "(1) identifying information needs and designing studies to develop needed information; (2) identifying and meaningfully discussing the issues raised by a particular proposed action; and (3) identifying and developing adequate mitigation for the impacts of a particular proposed action, or category of actions, on the State's coastal zone." The State did not officially object or concur in the letter per the requirements of 15 CFR 930.41.

- On May 16, 2007, MMS sent the CD's for CPA Lease Sale 205 to the States of Florida, Alabama, Mississippi, and Louisiana, documenting the consistency of the proposed sale with the CZM programs of those states. The State of Texas informed MMS that they no longer want to receive CPA lease sale CD's. In a July 2, 2007, letter, the State of Alabama concurred with MMS's CD and expressed support for the Blocks South of Baldwin County, Alabama Stipulation to address visual impacts. In a letter dated May 24, 2007, the State of Mississippi concurred with MMS's CD. In a letter dated July 12, 2007, the State of Florida stated it does not object to MMS's CD. In a letter dated July 13, 2007, the State of Louisiana requested a 15-day extension pursuant to 15 CFR 930.41(b). In a letter dated July 26, 2007, the State of Louisiana stated Sale 205 was consistent with the Louisiana Coastal Resources Program; however, the State identified issues of concern.

- On June 22, 2007, MMS published a Notice of Preparation of an EA on proposed Lease Sale 206. In the notice, MMS requested interested parties to submit comments regarding any new information or issues that should be addressed in the EA. One comment was received from the Governor of Alabama. The Governor requested that MMS provide reasonable and adequate protections for live-bottom areas, pinnacle reefs, chemosynthetic communities, and other sensitive features and areas, such as archeological sites off Alabama's coast that might be impacted by OCS-related oil and gas exploration and production activities in the CPA. The Governor requested that the Administration join with him "and other Governors, U.S. Senators, and Representatives, to work toward the enactment of new legislation to make additional revenue sharing with affected states, such as Alabama, a reality in the very near future."

- On July 24 and 26, 2007, public meetings were held to solicit comments regarding the Draft SEIS for EPA Lease Sale 224 in Pensacola, Florida, and Larose, Louisiana.

- On August 27, 2007, MMS published a Notice of Intent to Prepare an SEIS (NOI) on proposed Lease Sale 208, which will offer for sale approximately 5.8 million ac located in the southeastern part of the CPA ("181 South Area"). The SEIS will also address proposed oil and gas lease sales tentatively scheduled in 2009-2012 for the CPA and WPA. In the NOI, MMS requested interested parties to submit comments regarding any new information or issues that should be addressed in the SEIS. The comment period for the NOI closed on October 11, 2007.

Internal Scoping: Internal scoping is an ongoing activity for all environmental projects and NEPA documents. Part of internal scoping involves reviewing resource estimates and oil-spill modeling results used in the preparation of the Multisale EIS to determine if they are still valid. The MMS GOM Region's Office of Resource Evaluation reviewed the oil and gas resource projections and associated activities for CPA Lease Sale 206 and confirmed that they remain within the range of those projected by MMS for a "typical CPA lease sale." The MMS Headquarters' Oil-Spill Risk Analysis (OSRA) group confirmed that results from the OSRA model summarized in the Multisale EIS and presented in a separate MMS report (USDOI, MMS, 2007i) are still valid for the proposed lease sale.

Internal scoping also requires MMS subject matter experts/analysts and NEPA coordinators to continuously update their knowledge base and incorporate three primary informational components into their analyses:

(1) recent studies/reports;
(2) monitoring results; and
(3) related cumulative-impact data.

The MMS's analysts and coordinators take an active role in the preparation, execution, and peer review of studies and reports developed under MMS's Environmental Studies Program. In addition, some analysts provide expertise and are involved in additional studies and analyses conducted by other Federal/State agencies and universities concerning GOM issues and interests. The information obtained from these studies, as well as other relevant, non-MMS research, was considered by each subject matter expert in their assessment for this EA. Appendix C of the Multisale EIS lists the GOM Region's studies published from 2003 to 2006. Technical summaries for these studies are available on the MMS Internet website (http://www.gomr.mms.gov/homepg/regulate/environ/techsumm/rec_pubs.html).

Cumulative analyses are prepared by MMS subject matter experts that consider activities that could occur and may adversely affect GOM resources, including proposed CPA Lease Sale 206, prior and future OCS lease sales, State oil and gas activities, and other governmental and private projects and activities. The MMS analysts are often responsible for reviewing GOM activities not associated with oil and gas operations. All information gained from cumulative analyses was considered by MMS analysts in their assessments for this EA.

5.2. CONSULTATION AND COORDINATION CALENDAR

A complete description of all consultation and coordination activities and meetings is included in Chapter 5 of the Multisale EIS. A brief summary of these events follows:

Multisale EIS Process

March 7, 2006

The Notice of Intent (NOI) for the proposed 2007-2012 CPA and WPA lease sales was published in the *Federal Register*. A 45-day comment period was provided; it closed on April 21, 2006. Additional public notices were distributed via newspaper notices, mailed notices, and the Internet. The MMS received 65 scoping letters in response to the NOI, which are summarized in Chapter 5.3.1 of the Multisale EIS.

March 28-30, 2006
April 6, 2006

The MMS held scoping meetings in Houston, Texas; Harahan, Louisiana; Mobile, Alabama; and Tallahassee, Florida, to receive comments on the Draft EIS for the proposed 2007-2012 CPA and WPA lease sales. A summary of comments presented at the scoping meetings is provided in Chapter 5.3.1 of the Multisale EIS.

April 28, 2006

The Call for Information and Nominations (Call) for the proposed 2007-2012 lease sales was published in the *Federal Register*. A 30-day comment period was provided; it closed on May 30, 2006. The MMS received five comment letters in response to the Call, which are summarized in Chapter 5.3.3 of the Multisale EIS.

December 5-7, 2006

The MMS held public hearings in Houston, Texas; New Orleans and Larose, Louisiana; Panama City, Florida; and Mobile, Alabama, to receive comments on the Draft Multisale EIS for CPA Lease Sales 205, 206, 208, 213, 216, and 222, and WPA Lease Sales 204, 207, 210, 215, and 218. There were no speakers at the Houston, Mobile and Larose hearings. One individual presented comments at the New Orleans hearing and 26 at the Larose hearing. The comments are summarized in Chapter 5.5 of the Multisale EIS.

December 12, 2006

The EFH programmatic consultation was initiated and completed for the 2007-2012 lease sales, including Lease Sale 206. The NMFS concurred by letter dated December 12, 2006, that the information presented in the Draft Multisale EIS satisfies the EFH consultation procedures outlined in 50 CFR 600.920, and as specified in our March 17, 2000, findings. Provided MMS proposed mitigations, previous EFH conservation recommendations, and the standard lease stipulations and regulations are followed as proposed, NMFS agrees that impacts to EFH and associated fishery resources resulting from activities conducted under the 2007-2012 lease sales would be minimal. Therefore, unless future changes to the proposed 2007-2012 lease sales are proposed or new information becomes available, no further EFH consultation is required for the 2007-2012 lease sales.

June 28, 2007

The FWS and MMS have consulted informally per FWS guidance. A draft copy of the Biological Assessment, prepared by MMS, was submitted as requested by FWS (USDOI, MMS, 2007j). On June 28, 2007, MMS received oral confirmation from FWS that the consultation will remain informal; therefore there will be no new mitigations or Terms and Conditions from FWS. The final Biological Assessment and a request for a Letter of Concurrence were submitted to FWS on August 3, 2007. The FWS submitted a Letter of Concurrence dated September 14, 2007.

June 29, 2007

The NMFS BO was signed on June 29, 2007, and has been received by MMS. The BO concludes that the proposed lease sales and associated activities in the GOM in the 2007-2012 OCS Leasing Program, including Lease Sale 206, are not likely to jeopardize the continued existence of threatened and endangered species under NMFS jurisdiction, or destroy or adversely modify designated critical habitat. The NMFS issued an Incidental Take Statement on sea turtle species, which contains reasonable and prudent measures with implementing terms and conditions to help minimize take.

CPA Lease Sale 206 EA Process

June 22, 2007   The MMS published a Notice of Preparation of an EA on proposed CPA Lease Sale 206. In the notice, MMS requested interested parties to submit comments regarding any new information or issues that should be addressed in the EA. One comment was received from the Governor of Alabama.

6. REFERENCES

Ache, B. 2007. Written communication. National Oceanic and Atmospheric Administration. Email to the Gulf of Mexico Alliance Water Quality Team. Various emails sent in June 2007 in preparation for the annual July 2007 meeting.

Alabama Coastal Cleanup. 2007. Alabama's debris history. Internet website: http://www.alabamacoastalcleanup.com/debris-history. Accessed July 31, 2007.

American Gaming Association (AGA). 2003. State of the states: The AGA survey of casino entertainment. 32 pp. Internet website: http://www.americangaming.org/assets/files/AGA_survey_2003.pdf. Accessed July 9, 2007.

American Gaming Association (AGA). 2007. State of the states: The AGA survey of casino entertainment. Internet website: http://www.americangaming.org/survey/index.cfm. Accessed August 13, 2007.

American Petroleum Institute (API). 2006. Bulletin 2TD, Guidelines for tie-downs on offshore production facilities for the hurricane season, first edition. Internet website: http://www.api.org/Publications/2005-hurricane.cfm.

American Petroleum Institute (API). 2007. Gulf of Mexico MODU mooring practices for the 2007 hurricane season—interim recommendations. API Recommended Practice 95F, second edition, April 2007. Internet website: http://api-ec.api.org/Publications/upload/95F_2-3.pdf. 52 pp.

Ashton, P.K., R.A. Speir, and L.O. Upton III. 2004. Modeling exploration, development, and production in the Gulf of Mexico. Volumes I-III. U.S. Dept. of the Interior, Minerals Management Service, Environmental Studies Program, Herndon, VA. OCS Study MMS 2004-018.

Balseiro, A., A. Espi, I. Marquez, V. Perez, M.C. Ferreras, J.F. Garcia Marin, and J.M. Prieto. 2005. Pathological features in marine birds affected by the *Prestige*'s oil spill in the north of Spain. Journal of Wildlife Diseases 41:371-378.

Barras, J.A., S. Beville, D. Britsch, S. Hartley, S. Hawes, J. Johnston, P. Kemp, Q. Kinler, A. Martucci, J. Porthouse, D. Reed, K. Roy, S. Sapkota, and J. Suhayda. 2003. Historical and projected coastal Louisiana land changes: 1978-2050. USGS Open File Report 03-334.

Barras, J.A. 2006. Land area change in coastal Louisiana after the 2005 hurricanes: A series of three maps. USGS Open File Report 06-1274. U.S. Dept. of the Interior, Geological Survey.

Barras, J.A. 2007. Personal communication. Status of any further analysis of post-Katrina barrier island or mainland beach damages in Louisiana, Alabama, and Mississippi coasts. U.S. Dept. of the Interior, Geological Survey, National Wetlands Research Center, Lafayette, LA.

Barras, J.A. 2007. Satellite images and aerial photographs of the effects of Hurricanes Katrina and Rita on coastal Louisiana: USGS Data Series 281. Internet website: http://pubs.usgs.gov/ds/2007/281.

Barras, J.A. In press. Land area changes in coastal Louisiana after Hurricanes Katrina and Rita. In: Farris, G.S., G.J. Smith, M.P. Crane, C.R. Demas, L.L. Robbins, and D.L. Lavoie, eds. Science and the storms—The USGS response to the hurricanes of 2005. U.S. Dept. of the Interior, Geological Survey. Geological Survey Circular 1306. Internet website: http://pubs.usgs.gov/ds/2007/281/intro.htm.

Bass, A.S. and R.E. Turner. 1997. Relationships between salt marsh loss and dredge canals in three Louisiana estuaries. Journal of Coastal Research 13(3):895-903.

Bernier, J.C., R.A. Morton, and J.A. Barras. 2006. Constraining rates and trends of historical wetland loss, Mississippi River Delta Plain, south-central Louisiana. Coastal Environment and Water Quality, Water Resources Publications, LLC, Highlands Ranch, CO. Pp. 371-382. Internet website: http://coastal.er.usgs.gov/gc-subsidence/historical-wetland-loss.html.

Boesch, D.F., A. Mehta, J. Morris, W. Nuttle, C. Simenstad, and D. Swift. 1994. Scientific assessment of coastal wetland loss, restoration and management in Louisiana. Journal of Coastal Research 20:1-103.

Bolden, S. 2007. Personal communication. Information concerning the critical habitat and damage assessments of the Gulf sturgeon. U.S. Dept. of Commerce, NOAA Fisheries. May 9, 2007.

Bowles, A. 2007. Personal communication. Senior Research Biologist, Hubb-Sea World Research Institute, San Diego, CA. June 1, 2007.

Britsch, L.D. and J.B. Dunbar. 1993. Land-loss rates Louisiana coastal plain. Journal of Coastal Research 9:324-338.

Burger, A.E. 1993. Estimating the mortality of seabirds following oil spills: Effects of spill volume. Marine Pollution 26:140-143.

Burger, J. 1997. Oil spills. New Brunswick, NJ: Rutgers University Press. 261 pp.

Cahoon, D.R. Personal communication. 2007. Verification of pipeline and navigation canal erosion rates. U.S. Dept of the Interior, Geological Survey, Patuxent Wildlife Research Center. July 2007.

Church, R., D. Warren, R. Cullimore, L. Johnston, W. Schroeder, W. Patterson, T. Shirley. M. Kilgour, N. Morris, and J. Moore. 2007. Archaeological and biological analysis of World War II shipwrecks in the Gulf of Mexico: Artificial reef effect in deep water. U.S. Dept. of the Interior, Minerals Management Service, Gulf of Mexico OCS Region, New Orleans, LA. OCS Study MMS 2007-015. 387 pp.

Clark, R. 2007. Personal communication. Status of additional information or studies concerning post-Katrina storm damage to barrier islands and mainland beaches. Florida Dept. of Environmental Protection, Bureau of Beaches and Coastal Systems. May 2007.

Clark, R.R. and J.W. LaGrone. 2006. Hurricane Dennis & Hurricane Katrina: Final report on 2005 hurricane season impacts to northwest Florida. Florida Dept. of Environmental Protection, Division of Water Resource Management, Bureau of Beaches and Coastal Systems. 122 pp. Internet website: http://bcs.dep.state.fl.us/reports/2005/2005hurr.pdf. Accessed June 26, 2007.

Continental Shelf Associates, Inc. (CSA). 2007. Characterization of northern Gulf of Mexico deepwater hard-bottom communities with emphasis on *Lophelia* coral. U.S. Dept. of the Interior, Minerals Management Service, Gulf of Mexico OCS Region, New Orleans, LA. OCS Study MMS 2007-044. 169 pp. + app.

Dismukes, D. 2007. Personal communication. Louisiana State University, Center for Energy Studies, Baton Rouge, LA.

Dismukes, D.E., M. Barnett, D. Vitrano, and K. Strellec. 2007. Gulf of Mexico OCS oil and gas scenario examination: Onshore waste disposal. U.S. Dept. of the Interior, Minerals Management Service, Gulf of Mexico OCS Region, New Orleans, LA. OCS Report MMS 2007-051. 5 pp.

Dokken, Q.R., I.R. MacDonald, J.W. Tunnell, Jr., T. Wade, K. Withers, S.J. Dilworth, T.W. Bates, C.R. Beaver, and C.M. Rinaud. 2003. Long-term monitoring of the East and West Flower Garden Banks National Marine Sanctuary, 1998-2001: Final report. U.S. Dept. of the Interior, Minerals Management Service, Gulf of Mexico OCS Region, New Orleans, LA. OCS Study MMS 2003-031. 89 pp.

Federal Reserve Bank of Atlanta. 2006. Econ South. Volume 8, Number 4, Fourth Quarter 2006. Southeastern economy to grow modestly in 2007: State profiles–Louisiana. Louisiana continues march toward recovery – Louisiana employment: Better than the data suggest. Internet website: http://www.frbatlanta.org. Accessed June 14, 2007.

Flint, B. 2007. Personal communication. Wildlife Biologist, Pacific Remote Islands National Wildlife Refuge Complex, U.S. Dept. of the Interior, Fish and Wildlife Service, Honolulu, HI. June 11, 2007.

Florida Fish and Wildlife Commission. 2007. Fish and Wildlife Research Institute. Internet website: http://research.myfwc.com/features/view-article.asp?id=3261. Accessed May 29, 2007.

Florida State Dept. of Environmental Protection (FDEP). Bureau of Beaches and Coastal Systems. 2005. About beach and coastal data. April 20, 2005. Internet website: http://www.dep.state.fl.us/beaches/data/data.htm.

Florida State Dept. of Environmental Protection (FDEP). Bureau of Beaches and Coastal Systems. 2007. Beaches and coastal systems. August 31, 2007. Internet website: http://www.dep.state.fl.us/beaches/. Accessed June 28, 2007.

Gardner, J.V., P. Dartnell, and K.J. Sulak. 2002. Multibeam mapping of the pinnacles region, Gulf of Mexico. U.S. Dept. of the Interior, Geological Survey. USGS Open File Report OF02-006. Internet website: http://geopubs.wr.usgs.gov/open-file/of02-006/.

Geraci, J.R. and D.J. St. Aubin. 1980. Offshore petroleum resource development and marine mammals: A review and research recommendations. Marine Fisheries Review 42:1-12.

Geraci, J.R., and D.J. St. Aubin. 1987. Effects of offshore oil and gas development on marine mammals and turtles. In: Boesch, D.F. and N.N. Rabalais, eds. Long-term environmental effects of offshore oil and gas development. London: Elsevier Applied Science.

Google. 2007. Google advanced scholar search. Internet website: http://scholar.google.com/advanced_scholar_search?hl=en&lr=&ie=UTF-8. Accessed June 11, 2007.

Haig, S.H. and C.L. Ferland. 2002. 2001 international piping plover census. U.S. Dept. of the Interior, Geological Survey, Forest and Rangeland Ecosystem Science Center, Corvallis, OR. 293 pp.

Hall, D. 2006. U.S. Dept. of the Interior, Fish and Wildlife Service. Congressional testimony, Hurricane Katrina damage to USFWS refuges. Internet website: http://www.fws.gov/laws/Testimony/109th/2006/Dale%20Hall%20Impact%20of%20Hurrican%20Katrina%20on%20NWR%20march%2016%202006.htm.

Haney, J.L, Y. Wei, and S.G. Douglas. In preparation. Synthesis and integration of metrological/air quality data study. In preparartion for the U.S. Dept. of the Interior, Minerals Management Service, Gulf of Mexico OCS Region, New Orleans, LA, by ICF Consulting, San Rafael, CA. Contract no. 01-06-CT-39773.

Hardegree, B. 2007. Texas seagrass: Status, statewide issues, and restoration. Gulf of Mexico Alliance Regional Restoration Coordination Team Workshop, Galveston, TX. Internet website: http://www2.nos.noaa.gov/gomex/restoration/workshops/workshops.html.

Hartung, R. 1995. Assessment of the potential for long-term toxicological effects of the *Exxon Valdez* oil spill on birds and mammals. In: Wells, P.G., J.N.; Butler, and J.S. Hughes, eds. *Exxon Valdez* oil spill: Fate and effects in Alaskan waters. American Society for Testing and Materials, Philadelphia, PA. ASTM STP 1219.

Iledare, O.O. and M.J. Kaiser. 2007. Competition and performance in oil and gas lease sales and development in the U.S. Gulf of Mexico OCS region, 1983-1999. U.S. Dept. of the Interior, Minerals Management Service, Gulf of Mexico OCS Region, New Orleans, La. OCS Study MMS 2007-034. 106 pp.

Jankowski, M. 2007. Personal communication. Wildlife Disease Specialist, U.S. Dept. of the Interior, USGS/BRD, National Wildlife Health Center, Madison, WI. June 6, 2007.

Khan, R.A. and P. Ryan. 1991. Long-term effects of crude oil on common murres (*Uria aalge*) following rehabilitation. Bulletin of Environmental Contamination and Toxicology 46:216-222.

Kirkham, C. 2007. Storms muddy waters for La. fishers. *The Times-Picayune*, New Orleans, LA. May 20, 2007. Internet website: http://blog.nola.com/times-picayune/2007/05/storms_muddy_waters_for_la_fis.html.

Leadon, M.E. 2004. Hurricane Ivan: Beach and dune erosion and structural damage assessment and post-storm recovery plan for the Panhandle Coast of Florida. Florida Dept. of Environmental Protection, Division of Water Resources Management, Bureau of Beaches and Coastal Systems. 64 pp. Internet website: http://bcs.dep.state.fl.us/reports/ivan.pdf. Accessed June 28, 2007.

Leblanc, D. 2007. Personal communication. Biologist, U.S. Dept. of the Interior, Fish and Wildlife Service, Ecological Services, Daphne, AL. June 25, 2007.

Logan, J.R. 2007. The impact of Katrina: Race and class in storm-damaged neighborhoods. Brown University, Providence, RI. 16 pp. Internet website: http://www.s4.brown.edu/Katrina/report.pdf. Accessed July 10, 2007.

Louis Berger Group, Inc. 2004. OCS-related infrastructure in the Gulf of Mexico fact book. U.S. Dept. of the Interior, Minerals Management Service, Gulf of Mexico OCS Region, New Orleans, LA. OCS Study MMS 2004-027. 234 pp.

Louisiana Coastal Wetlands Conservation and Restoration Task Force. 1993. Coastal Wetland Planning, Protection, and Restoration Act: Louisiana coastal wetlands restoration plan; main report and environmental impact statement. Louisiana Coastal Wetlands Conservation and Restoration Task Force, Baton Rouge, LA.

Louisiana Dept. of Environmental Quality (LADEQ). 2007a. Water quality assessment in Louisiana. Internet website: http://www.deq.louisiana.gov/portal/Default.aspx?tabid=69. Accessed July 5, 2007.

Louisiana Dept. of Environmental Quality (LADEQ). 2007b. Beach sweep & inland waterway cleanup. Louisiana Dept. of Environmental Quality, Division of Environmental Assistance. Internet website: http://www.deq.louisiana.gov/portal/default.aspx?tabid=191. Accessed July 31, 2007.

Louisiana Dept. of Wildlife and Fisheries. 2007. Estimates indicate Katrina and Rita could cost the State's fisheries' industries $2.3 billion. Internet website: http://www.louisianaseafood.com/news.cfm?ArticleID=126. Accessed July 10, 2007.

Louisiana Universities Marine Consortium (LUMCON). 2007a. Hypoxia in the northern Gulf of Mexico. Internet website: http://www.gulfhypoxia.net/. Accessed July 5, 2007.

Louisiana Universities Marine Consortium (LUMCON). 2007b. Dead zone size near top end. Press Release, July 28, 2007. Internet website: http://www.gulfhypoxia.net/shelfwide07/PressRelease07.pdf. Accessed July 30, 2007.

Maiaro, J.L. 2007. Disturbance effects on nekton communities of seagrasses and bare substrates in Biloxi Marsh, Louisiana. Master's thesis, Louisiana State University, Baton Rouge, LA. 78 pp. Internet website: http://etd.lsu.edu/docs/available/etd-07032007-101237/unrestricted/Maiaro_thesis.pdf.

May, C.A. 2007. Distribution, status, and trends of seagrasses in Mississippi. Gulf of Mexico Alliance Regional Restoration Coordination Team Workshop, March 6-9, 2007, Spanish Fort, AL. 15 pp. Internet website: http://www2.nos.noaa.gov/gomex/restoration/workshops/workshops.html.

Maze-Foley, K. and K. Mullin. 2006. Cetaceans of the oceanic northern Gulf of Mexico: Distributions, group sizes and interspecific associations. Journal of Cetacean Research and Management 8(2):203-213.

Mississippi Alabama Sea Grant Consortium. 2007. Mississippi coastal cleanup. Internet website: http://www.masgc.org/cleanup/index.htm. Accessed July 31, 2007.

Mississippi Gulf Coast Convention & Visitors Bureau. 2007. Gulf Coast gaming revenues. Internet website: http://www.gulfcoast.org/static/index.cfm?contentID=329. Accessed July 9, 2007.

Morton, B. 2007. Personal communication. Request for new post-Katrina storm damage information concerning Florida barrier islands and mainland beaches. U.S. Dept. of Interior, Geological Survey, Integrated Science Center, St. Petersburg, FL. May 2007.

Nicholls, J.L. and G.A. Baldassarre. 1990. Habitat associations of piping plovers wintering in the United States. Wilson Bulletin 102:581-590.

Nisbet, I.C.T. 2007. Personal communication. Chief, I.C.T. Nisbet & Co., North Falmouth, MA. June 4, 2007.

OCLC FirstSearch. 2007. Internet website: http://newfirstsearch.oclc.org/. Accessed June 11, 2007.

Palka, D. and M. Johnson, eds. 2007. Cooperative research to study dive patterns of sperm whales in the Atlantic Ocean. U.S. Dept. of the Interior, Minerals Management Service, Gulf of Mexico OCS Region, New Orleans, LA. OCS Study MMS 2007-033. 49 pp.

Parsons, K.C. 1994. The *Arthur Kill* oil spills: Biological effects in birds. In: Burger, J., ed. Before and after an oil spill: The *Arthur Kill*. New Brunswick, NJ: Rutgers University Press. Pp. 215-237.

Paruka, F. 2007. Personal communication. Information concerning the critical habitat, sampling programs, and damage assessments of the Gulf sturgeon. U.S. Dept. of the Interior, Fish and Wildlife Service, Ecological Services, Fisheries Resource Office, Panama City FL. May 29, 2007.

PBS&J. In preparation. Impacts of recent hurricane activity on historic shipwrecks in the Gulf of Mexico. In preparartion for the U.S. Dept. of the Interior, Minerals Management Service, Gulf of Mexico OCS Region, New Orleans, LA, by PBS&J, Austin, TX. Contract no. M07PC13010.

Penland, S., L. Wayne, L.D. Britsch, S.J. Williams, A.D. Beall, and V. Caridas Butterworth. 2001a. Geomorphic classification of coastal land loss between 1932 and 1990 in the Mississippi River Delta Plain, southeastern Louisiana. U.S. Dept. of the Interior, Geological Survey, Coastal and Marine Geology Program, Woods Hole Field Center, Woods Hole, MA. Open File Report 00-417.

Penland, S., L. Wayne, L.D. Britsch, S. J. Williams, A. D. Beall, and V. Caridas Butterworth. 2001b. Process classification of coastal land loss between 1932 and 1990 in the Mississippi River Delta Plain, southeastern Louisiana. U.S. Dept. of the Interior, Geological Survey, Coastal and Marine Geology Program, Woods Hole Field Center, Woods Hole, MA. Open File Report 00-418.

Precht, W.F., R.B. Aronson, K.J.P. Deslarzes, M.L. Robbart, A. Gelber, and B. Zimmer. 2006. Long-term monitoring at the East and West Flower Garden Banks, 2002-2003: Final report. U.S. Dept. of the Interior, Minerals Management Service, Gulf of Mexico OCS Region, New Orleans, LA. OCS Study MMS 2006-035. 182pp.

Precht, W.F., R.B. Aronson, K.J.P. Deslarzes, M.L. Robbart, A. Gelber., and B. Gearheart. In preparation (a). Post-hurricane assessment of sensitive habitats of the Flower Garden Banks vicinity: Draft report. U.S. Dept. of the Interior, Minerals Management Service, Gulf of Mexico OCS Region, New Orleans, LA.

Precht, W.F., R.B. Aronson, K.J.P. Deslarzes, M.L. Robbart, A. Gelber, and B. Zimmer. In preparation (b). Long-term monitoring at the East and West Flower Garden Banks, 2004: Final report. U.S. Dept. of the Interior, Minerals Management Service, Gulf of Mexico OCS Region, New Orleans, LA.

Rice, S.D., J.F. Karinen, and C.C. Brodersen. 1983. Effects of oiled sediment on juvenile king crab. U.S. Dept. of Commerce, National Oceanic and Atmospheric Administration, National Marine Fisheries Service, Northwest and Alaska Fisheries Center, Auke Bay Laboratory, Auke Bay, AK. Internet website: http://www.gomr.mms.gov/PI/PDFImages/ESPIS/0/976.pdf.

Rooker, J.R., R.T. Kraus, and R.L. Hill. In preparation. Spatial and temporal patterns of recruitment to mid- and outer-shelf banks in the NW Gulf of Mexico. Unpublished preliminary report. Texas A&M University, College Station, TX.

Rowley K. 2007. GulfGov reports: A year and a half after Katrina and Rita, an uneven recovery. Nelson A. Rockefeller Institute of Government, Albany, NY, and Public Affairs Research Council of Louisiana, Baton Rouge, LA. 73 pp. Internet website: http://www.rockinst.org/WorkArea/showcontent.aspx?id=9920.

Scaife, W.B., R.E. Turner, and R. Costanza. 1983. Recent land loss and canal impacts in coastal Louisiana. Environmental Management 7:433-442.

Schroeder, W.W. 2007. Seafloor characteristics and distribution patterns of *Lophelia pertusa* and other sessile megafauna at two upper-slope site sin the northeastern Gulf of Mexico. U.S. Dept. of the Interior, Minerals Management Service, Gulf of Mexico OCS Region, New Orleans, LA. OCS Study MMS 2007-035. 49 pp.

Scott, L. 2007. Advancing in the aftermath: Tracking the recovery from Katrina and Rita. Internet website: http://www.Lorencscottassociates.com. Accessed July 2, 2007.

Shigenaka, G. 2001. Toxicity of oil to reef-building corals: A spill response perspective. U.S. Dept. of Commerce, National Oceanic and Atmospheric Administration, Seattle, WA. NOAA Technical Memorandum NOS OR&R 8. 95 pp. Internet website: http://archive.orr.noaa.gov/oilaids/coral/pdfs/coral_tox.pdf.

Slack, T. 2007. Personal communication. Information concerning the State of Mississippi Gulf sturgeon sampling and tagging program. Mississippi State Museum of Natural History. June 4, 2007.

Smith, R. 2007. Personal communication. 2006 international bird census. U.S. Dept. of the Interior, Fish and Wildlife Service, Ecological Services Office, Lafayette, LA.

Smultea, M. and B. Würsig. 1995. Bottlenose dolphin reactions to the *Mega Borg* oil spill. Aquatic Mammals 21:171-181.

Sneckenberger, S. 2007. Personal communication. Biologist, U.S. Dept. of the Interior, Fish and Wildlife Service, Ecological Services, Panama City, FL. July 16, 2007.

Spalding, E.A. and M.W. Hester. 2007. Interactive effects of hydrology and salinity on oligohaline plant species productivity: Implications of relative sea-level rise. Estuaries and Coasts 30(2):214-225. Internet website: http://erf.org/cesn/vol30n2r4.html.

State of Louisiana. Coastal Protection and Restoration Authority (CPRA). 2007. Integrated ecosystem restoration and hurricane protection: Louisiana's comprehensive master plan for a sustainable coast. 140 pp. Internet website: http://www.lacpra.org/assets/docs/cprafinalreport_pg77_pg85_5-2-07.pdf.

Systems Applications International, Sonoma Technology, Inc., Earth Tech, Alpine Geophysics, and A.T. Kearney. 1995. Gulf of Mexico air quality study: Final report. Volumes I-III. U.S. Dept. of the Interior, Minerals Management Service, Gulf of Mexico OCS Region, New Orleans, LA. OCS Study MMS 95-0038, 95-0039, and 95-0040. 650, 214, and 190 pp., respectively.

Tenaglia, K.M., J.L. Van Zant, and M.C. Wooten. 2007. Genetic relatedness and spatial associations of jointly captured Alabama beach mice (*Peromyscus polionotus ammobates*). Journal of Mammalogy 88:580-588.

Terrell, D. and R. Bilbo. 2007. A report on the impact of Hurricanes Katrina and Rita on Louisiana businesses: 2005Q2-2006Q2. Louisiana State University, Division of Economic Development, Baton Rouge, LA. 51 pp. Internet website: http://www.bus.lsu.edu/centers/ded/ or http://www.bus.lsu.edu/centers/ded/reports/2006Q4_Business_Report.pdf/.

Texas Commission on Environmental Quality. 2007. Texas Commission on Environmental Quality. Internet website: http://www.tceq.state.tx.us/. Accessed July 5, 2007.

Texas General Land Office (TGLO). 2007. Coastal Coordination Division. Internet website: http://www.glo.state.tx.us/coastal/pubs.html. Accessed July 9, 2007.

Tolbert, C.M. 1995. Oil and gas development and coastal income inequality: A comparative analysis. U.S. Dept. of the Interior, Minerals Management Service, Gulf of Mexico OCS Region, New Orleans, LA.. OCS Study MMS 94-0052. 75 pp. [MMS updated certain information in this study: Tolbert, 2006.]

Tolbert, C.M. II, ed. 2006. Sustainable community in oil and gas country: Final report. U.S. Dept. of the Interior, Minerals Management Service, Gulf of Mexico OCS Region, New Orleans, LA.. OCS Study MMS 2006-011. 76 pp.

Travel Industry Association of America. 2003. 2002 TravelScope profile of U.S. travelers to Louisiana. The Research Department of the Travel Industry Association of America, Washington, DC. July 2003.

Travel Industry Association of America. 2004. 2003 TravelScope profile of U.S. travelers to Louisiana. The Research Department of the Travel Industry Association of America. Washington, DC. July 2004.

Travel Industry Association of America. 2005. 2004 TravelScope profile of U.S. travelers to Louisiana. The Research Department of the Travel Industry Association of America. Washington, DC. June 2005.

Tremplay, T. 2007. Personal communication. Request for current information concerning post-Katrina storm damage to Texas barrier islands and beaches. Texas Bureau of Economic Geology, Austin, TX. May 2007.

Turner, R.E., R. Costanza, and W. Scaife. 1982. Canals and wetland erosion rates in coastal Louisiana. In: Conference on Coastal Erosion and Wetland Modification in Louisiana: Causes, Consequences, and Options. U.S. Dept. of the Interior, Fish and Wildlife Service, Office of Biological Services. FWS/OBS 82/59.

Upton, L.O. III and P.K. Ashton. 2005. Measuring the impact of high oil prices and Federal policy initiatives in offshore Gulf of Mexico exploration, development, and production activity. Innovation & Information Consultants, Inc. Presentation, 25th Annual North American Conference of the United States Association for Energy Economics/International Association for Energy Economics, September 18-21, 2005, Denver CO. 16 pp. Internet website: http://www.iaee.org/documents/denver/upton.pdf.

U.S. Dept. of Commerce. Bureau of the Census. 2007. County business patterns. EPCD. Internet website: http://www.census.gov/epcd/cbp/view/cbpview.html. Accessed August 13-17, 2007.

U.S. Dept. of Commerce. National Marine Fisheries Service. 2005. National survey on recreation and the environment (NSRE). Internet website: http://marineeconomics.noaa.gov/NSRE/welcome.html. Accessed August 23, 2007.

U.S. Dept. of Commerce. National Marine Fisheries Service. 2007a. Endangered Species Act Section 7 consultation on the effects of the five-year outer continental shelf oil and gas leasing program (2007-2012) in the Central and Western Planning Areas of the Gulf of Mexico. Biological Opinion. June 29. F/SER/2006/02611. 127 pp.

U.S. Dept. of Commerce. National Marine Fisheries Service. 2007b. Report to Congress on the impact of Hurricanes Katrina, Rita, and Wilma on commercial and recreational fishery habitat of Alabama, Florida, Louisiana, Mississippi, and Texas. July 2007. 191 pp. + apps. Internet website: http://ecowatch.ncddc.noaa.gov/nmfs-report.

U.S. Dept. of Commerce. National Marine Fisheries Service. 2007c. Fish stock sustainability index (FSSI): Summary of stock status determination changes from April 1, 2007 through June 30, 2007. Status of U.S. fisheries, second quarter update, July 17, 2007. 2 pp. Internet website: http://www.nmfs.noaa.gov/sfa/domes_fish/StatusoFisheries/2007/SecondQuarter/Q2-2007-FSSISummaryChanges.pdf.

U.S. Dept. of Commerce. National Marine Fisheries Service. 2007d. Office of Science and Technology. Fisheries of the United States 2006 119 pp. Internet website: http://www.st.nmfs.gov/st1/fus/fus06/fus_2006.pdf. Accessed July 31, 2007.

U.S. Dept. of Commerce. National Marine Fisheries Service. 2007e. Marine recreational fisheries statistics survey, Gulf of Mexico. Internet website: http://www.st.nmfs.gov/st1/recreational/index.html. Accessed August 9, 2007.

U.S. Dept. of Commerce. National Marine Fisheries Service. 2007f. National survey on recreation and the environment (NSRE). Internet website: http://marineeconomics.noaa.gov/NSRE/. Accessed July 3, 2007.

U.S. Dept. of Commerce. National Oceanic and Atmospheric Administration. 2007. Gulf of Mexico Marine Debris Project. Internet website: http://gulfofmexico.marinedebris.noaa.gov/. Accessed July 11, 2007.

U.S. Dept. of Commerce. National Oceanic and Atmospheric Administration. Office of Response and Restoration. 2007. Summary points: 10 years of intertidal monitoring after the *Exxon Valdez* spill. Internet website: http://archive.orr.noaa.gov/bat/10years.html. Accessed September 11, 2007.

U.S. Dept. of Labor. Bureau of Labor Statistics. 2006. Review: Special issue, Hurricane Katrina. August 2006, Vol. 129, No. 8. 78 pp.

U.S. Dept. of Labor. Bureau of Labor Statistics. 2007. News. U.S. Dept. of Labor, Washington DC. USDL 07-0713. May 18, 2007.

U.S. Dept. of the Army. Corps of Engineers. 2004. Louisiana coastal area (LCA): Ecosystem restoration study. Volumes I and II. Draft programmatic environmental impact statement. U.S. Dept. of the Army, Corps of Engineers, New Orleans District, New Orleans, LA.

U.S. Dept. of the Interior, Fish and Wildlife Service and U.S. Dept. of Commerce, Bureau of the Census. 2001. National survey of fishing, hunting, and wildlife-associated recreation. U.S. Dept. of the Interior, Fish and Wildlife Service, Washington, DC. 170 pp.

U.S. Dept. of the Interior. Fish and Wildlife Service. 2007a. Bald eagle soars off endangered species list. News Release, June 28, 2007. 3 pp. Internet website: http://www.fws.gov/migratorybirds/issues/BaldEagle/FINALEagle%20release.pdf. Accessed July 24, 2007.

U.S. Dept. of the Interior. Fish and Wildlife Service. 2007b. Gulf sturgeon recovery. Internet website: http://www.fws.gov/panamacity/programs/gulfsturg-recov.html. Accessed May 29, 2007.

U.S. Dept. of the Interior. Fish and Wildlife Service. 2007c. Critical habitat of the Gulf sturgeon. Internet website: http://www.fws.gov/alabama/gs. Accessed May 29, 2007.

U.S. Dept. of the Interior. Fish and Wildlife Service. 2007d. National survey of fishing, hunting, and wildlife-associated recreation. Internet website: http://federalaid.fws.gov/surveys/surveys.html. Assessed on July 31, 2007.

U.S. Dept. of the Interior. Geological Survey. 1988. Report to Congress: Coastal barrier resource system. Recommendations for additions to or deletions from the Coastal Barrier Resource System. Vol. 18, Louisiana.

U.S. Dept. of the Interior. Geological Survey. 2003. Pinnacles deep reefs. U.S. Dept. of the Interior, Geological Survey, Florida Integrated Science Center. Internet website: http://cars.er.usgs.gov/coastaleco/Pinnacles_Deep_Reefs/_pinnacles_deep_reefs.html.

U.S. Dept. of the Interior. Geological Survey. 2006. Extreme storm impact studies. Internet website: http://coastal.er.usgs.gov/hurricanes. Accessed June 25, 2007.

U.S. Dept. of the Interior. Geological Survey. 2007a. Hurricane Katrina impact studies. Internet website: http://coastal.er.usgs.gov/hurricanes/katrina. Accessed June 22, 2007.

U.S. Dept. of the Interior. Geological Survey. 2007b. Long-term wetland change Florida. Internet website: http://coastal.er.usgs.gov/wetlands/. Accessed June 20, 2007.

U.S. Dept. of the Interior. Geological Survey. 2007c. USGS reports latest land change estimates for Louisiana coast. Internet website: http://www.peoplelandandwater.gov/usgs/usgs_02-20-07_usgs-reports-latest.cfm. Accessed July 10, 2007.

U.S. Dept. of the Interior. Geological Survey. 2007d. Gulf of Mexico and southeast tidal wetlands. Internet website: http://coastal.er.usgs.gov/wetlands/. Accessed June 27, 2007.

U.S. Dept. of the Interior. Geological Survey. 2007e. USGS Publications Warehouse. Internet website: http://pubs.er.usgs.gov/usgspubs. Accessed June 27,2007.

U.S. Dept. of the Interior. Minerals Management Service. 2001. Outer continental shelf oil & gas leasing program: 2002-2007—draft environmental impact statement. 2 vols. U.S. Dept. of the Interior, Minerals Management Service, Herndon, VA. OCS EIS/EA 2001-079.

U.S. Dept. of the Interior. Minerals Management Service. 2006. Investigations of chemosynthetic communities on the lower continental shelf of the Gulf of Mexico. Ongoing study co-funded by U.S. Dept. of the Interior, Minerals Management Service and U.S. Dept. of Commerce, NOAA, Office of Ocean Exploration. Internet website for the study profile: http://www.gomr.mms.gov/homepg/regulate/environ/ongoing_studies/gm/GM-05-03.html. Internet website for the *Alvin* cruise from May 7-June 2: http://oceanexplorer.noaa.gov/explorations/06mexico/welcome.html.

U.S. Dept. of the Interior. Minerals Management Service. 2007a. Gulf of Mexico OCS oil and gas lease sales: 2007-2012; Western Planning Area Sales 204, 207, 210, 215, and 218; Central Planning Area Sales 205, 206, 208, 213, 216, and 222—final environmental impact statement. 2 vols. U.S. Dept. of the Interior, Minerals Management Service, Gulf of Mexico OCS Region, New Orleans, LA. OCS EIS/EA MMS 2007-018.

U.S. Dept. of the Interior. Minerals Management Service. 2007b. Outer continental shelf oil and gas leasing program, 2007-2012. U.S. Dept. of the Interior, Minerals Management Service, Washington, DC.

U.S. Dept. of the Interior. Minerals Management Service. 2007c. Outer continental shelf oil and gas leasing program: 2007-2012—final environmental impact statement. 2 vols. U.S. Dept. of the Interior, Minerals Management Service, Herndon, VA. OCS EIS/EA MMS 2007-003.

U.S. Dept. of the Interior. Minerals Management Service. 2007d. Gulf of Mexico OCS oil and gas scenario examination: Exploration and development activity. U.S. Dept. of the Interior, Minerals Management Service, Gulf of Mexico OCS Region, New Orleans, LA. OCS Report MMS 2007-052. 14 pp.

U.S. Dept. of the Interior. Minerals Management Service. 2007e. Gulf of Mexico OCS oil and gas scenario examination: Pipeline landfalls. U.S. Dept. of the Interior, Minerals Management Service, Gulf of Mexico OCS Region, New Orleans, LA. OCS Report MMS 2007-053. 5pp.

U.S. Dept. of Interior. Minerals Management Service. 2007f. Petroleum spills of one barrel or greater from Federal Outer Continental Shelf facilities resulting from damages caused by 2005 Hurricanes Katrina and Rita including post-hurricane seepage through June 2007. Internet website: http://www.mms.gov/incidents/PDFs/HurrKatrinaRitaSpillageRev30Jul2007.pdf. Assessed July 30, 2007.

U.S. Dept. of the Interior. Minerals Management Service. 2007g. Estimated petroleum spillage from facilities associated with Federal Outer Continental Shelf (OCS) oil and gas activities resulting from damages caused by Hurricanes Rita and Katrina in 2005. U.S. Dept. of the Interior, Minerals Management Service, Herndon, VA. Internet website: http://www.mms.gov/incidents/PDFs/HurrKatrinaRitaSpillageRev25Jan2007Final.pdf. Accessed February 1, 2007.

U.S. Dept. of the Interior. Minerals Management Service. 2007h. Minerals Management Service marks hurricane season 2007. News Release, August 30, 2007. U.S. Dept. of the Interior, Minerals Management Service, Gulf of Mexico Region, New Orleans, LA. Internet website: http://www.gomr.mms.gov/homepg/whatsnew/newsreal/2007/070530.pdf.

U.S. Dept. of the Interior. Minerals Management Service. 2007i. Oil-spill risk analysis: Gulf of Mexico Outer Continental Shelf (OCS) lease sales, Central Planning Area and Western Planning Area, 2007-

2012 and Gulfwide OCS Program, 2007-2046. U.S. Dept. of the Interior, Minerals Management Service, Washington, DC. OCS Report MMS 2007-040.

U.S. Dept. of the Interior. Minerals Management Service. 2007j. Biological assessment, USFWS consultation, Gulf of Mexico OCS oil and gas lease sales: 2007-2012. U.S. Dept. of the Interior, Minerals Management Service, Gulf of Mexico OCS Region, New Orleans, LA.

U.S. Dept. of the Interior. Minerals Management Service. In preparation. Five-year meteorological database for the OCD and CALPUFF models. Internet website: http://www.gomr.mms.gov/homepg/regulate/environ/ongoing_studies/gm/52847.html.

U.S. Dept. of the Interior. National Park Service. 2005. November 2005 archeology e-gram. Internet website: http://www.nps.gov/archeology/pubs/egrams/0511.pdf. Accessed July 30, 2007.

U.S. Environmental Protection Agency. 2005. Ozone nonattainment state/area/county report, September 29, 2005. Internet website: http://www.epa.gov/oar/oaqps/greenbk/gncs.html.

U.S. Environmental Protection Agency. 2007a. Phase 2 of the final rule to implement the 8-hour ozone national ambient air quality standard. Final notice of reconsideration. *Federal Register* 72 FR 110, Pp. 31727-31749.

U.S. Environmental Protection Agency. 2007b. 8-hour ozone nonattainment state/area/county report. As of June 20, 2007. Internet website: http://www.epa.gov/oar/oaqps/greenbk/gncs.html.

U.S. Environmental Protection Agency. 2007c. Particulate matter (PM-2.5) nonattainment state/area/county report. As of June 20, 2007. Internet website: http://www.epa.gov/oar/oaqps/greenbk/qncs.html#ALABAMA.

U.S. Environmental Protection Agency. 2007d. Offshore and oil & gas NPDES permits, Region 6. Internet website: http://www.epa.gov/Arkansas/6en/w/offshore/home.htm. Accessed July 2, 2007.

U.S. Environmental Protection Agency. 2007e. Oil & gas NPDES permits in the Southeast Region 4. Internet website: http://www.epa.gov/Region4/water/permits/oil&gas.html. Accessed July 3, 2007.

U.S. Environmental Protection Agency. 2007f. National estuary program coastal condition report -- NEP CCR. Internet website: http://www.epa.gov/owow/oceans/nepccr/index.html. Accessed July 3, 2007.

U.S. Environmental Protection Agency. 2007g. USEPA Region 6 NPDES OCS General Permit No. GMG290000. Internet website: http://www.epa.gov/earth1r6/6wq/npdes/genpermt/index.htm. Accessed July 2, 2007.

Veil, J., T.A. Kimmell, and A.C. Rechner. 2005. Characteristics of produced water discharged to the Gulf of Mexico hypoxic zone. U.S. Dept. of Energy, National Energy Technology Laboratory.

Velando, A., I. Munilla, and P.M. Leyenda. 2005. Short-term indirect effects of the 'Prestige' oil spill on European shags: Changes in availability of prey. Marine Ecology Progress Series 302:263-274.

Vittor, B.A. 2007. SAV and wetlands status and trends in coastal Alabama. Gulf of Mexico Alliance Regional Restoration Coordination Team Workshop,, Spanish Fort, AL. Internet website: http://www2.nos.noaa.gov/gomex/restoration/workshops/workshops.html.

Walther, D. 2007. Personal communication. Information concerning the status of Gulf sturgeon in the Pearl River, Louisiana, watershed. U.S. Dept. of the Interior, Fish and Wildlife Service, Ecological Services Field Office, Lafayette, LA. May 29, 2007.

Weaver, D.C., G.D. Dennis III, and K.J. Sulak. 2001. Northeastern Gulf of Mexico coastal and marine ecosystem program: Community structure and trophic ecology of demersal fishes on the Pinnacles Reef tract; final synthesis report. U.S. Dept. of the Interior, Geological Survey, USGS BSR-2001-0008 and Minerals Management Service, Gulf of Mexico OCS Region, New Orleans, LA, OCS Study MMS-2002-034. 92 pp. + apps.

White, W.A., T.A. Tremblay, R.L. Waldinger, T.L. Hepner, and T.R. Calnan. 2005. Status and trends of wetland and aquatic habitats on barrier islands, Freeport to East Matagorda Bay and South Padre Island. Texas General Land Office, Coastal Coordination Division. Internet website: http://www.glo.state.tx.us/coastal/statustrends/freeport-spi/index.html. Accessed June 19, 2007.

White, W.A., T.A. Tremblay, R.L. Waldinger, and T.R. Calnan. 2007. Status of wetlands and aquatic habitats on Texas barriers: Upper Coast Strand Plain Chenier System and Southern Coast Padre Island National Seashore. April 2007. Texas General Land Office, Coastal Coordination Division. Internet website: http://www.glo.state.tx.us/coastal/statustrends/chenier-pins/index.html. Accessed July 9 2007.

Wilson, D.L., J.N. Fanjoy, and R.S. Billings. 2004. Gulfwide emission inventory study for the regional haze and ozone modeling efforts: Final report. U.S. Dept. of the Interior, Minerals Management Service, Gulf of Mexico OCS Region, New Orleans, LA. OCS Study 2004-072. 273 pp.

Wilson, S. 2007. Personal communication. Information concerning the reissued NPDES general permit. USEPA, Region 6. July 13, 2007.

Woods & Poole Economics, Inc. 2006. The 2006 complete economic and demographic data source (CEDDS) on CD-ROM.

Woods & Poole Economics, Inc. 2007. The 2007 complete economic and demographic data source (CEDDS) on CD-ROM.

7. PREPARERS

Dennis L. Chew, Chief, Environmental Assessment Section
Gary D. Goeke, NEPA/CZM Unit Supervisor, Supervisory Environmental Protection Specialist

Michelle V. Morin, Coordinator, Senior Environmental Scientist
Casey Rowe, Coordinator, Senior Environmental Scientist
Mary C. Boatman, Headquarters' Coordinator, Environmental Specialist

Dave Ball, Marine Archaeologist
Gregory S. Boland, Fisheries Biologist/Biological Oceanographer
Carole L. Current, Physical Oceanographer
Donald (Tre) W. Glenn, III, Protected Species Biologist
Mike Gravois, Geographer
Larry M. Hartzog, Environmental Scientist
Tim Holder, Social Scientist
Nancy M. Kornrumpf, Program Analyst
Jill Leale, Geographer
Daniel (Herb) Leedy, Supervisor, Biological Sciences Unit
Harry Luton, Social Scientist
Stacie Merritt, Meteorologist
Margaret Metcalf, Physical Scientist
Deborah H. Miller, Technical Publications Editor
Tara Montgomery, Supervisor, Mapping and Automation Unit
David P. Moran, Environmental Scientist
Carol Roden, Protected Species Biologist
John L. Rodi, Leasing Program Manager
Catherine A. Rosa, Environmental Assessment Program Specialist
James Sinclair, Marine Biologist
Kristen L. Strellec, Economist

The Department of the Interior Mission

As the Nation's principal conservation agency, the Department of the Interior has responsibility for most of our nationally owned public lands and natural resources. This includes fostering sound use of our land and water resources; protecting our fish, wildlife, and biological diversity; preserving the environmental and cultural values of our national parks and historical places; and providing for the enjoyment of life through outdoor recreation. The Department assesses our energy and mineral resources and works to ensure that their development is in the best interests of all our people by encouraging stewardship and citizen participation in their care. The Department also has a major responsibility for American Indian reservation communities and for people who live in island territories under U.S. administration.

The Minerals Management Service Mission

As a bureau of the Department of the Interior, the Minerals Management Service's (MMS) primary responsibilities are to manage the mineral resources located on the Nation's Outer Continental Shelf (OCS), collect revenue from the Federal OCS and onshore Federal and Indian lands, and distribute those revenues.

Moreover, in working to meet its responsibilities, the **Offshore Minerals Management Program** administers the OCS competitive leasing program and oversees the safe and environmentally sound exploration and production of our Nation's offshore natural gas, oil and other mineral resources. The MMS **Minerals Revenue Management** meets its responsibilities by ensuring the efficient, timely and accurate collection and disbursement of revenue from mineral leasing and production due to Indian tribes and allottees, States and the U.S. Treasury.

The MMS strives to fulfill its responsibilities through the general guiding principles of: (1) being responsive to the public's concerns and interests by maintaining a dialogue with all potentially affected parties and (2) carrying out its programs with an emphasis on working to enhance the quality of life for all Americans by lending MMS assistance and expertise to economic development and environmental protection.